POETRY SKETCHES
A PEACE CORPS MEMOIR

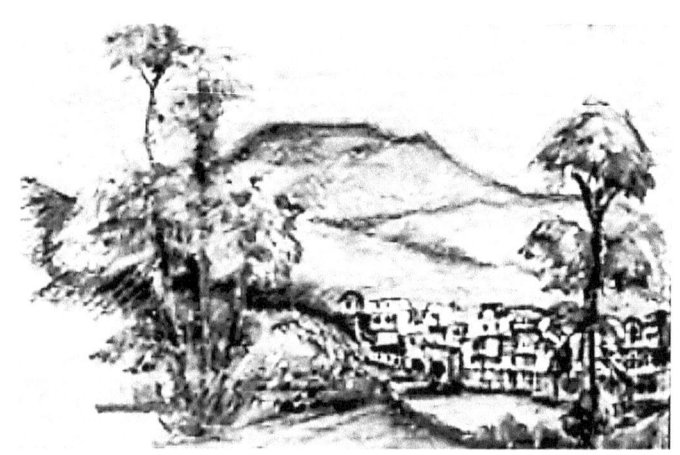

Mount Hakim Dominates Harar

POETRY SKETCHES
A PEACE CORPS MEMOIR

A Personal Journey
through Poetry and Art

———————————

Eldon Katter

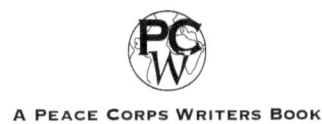

A PEACE CORPS WRITERS BOOK

POETRY SKETCHES: A PEACE CORPS MEMOIR

A Peace Corps Writers Book — an imprint of Peace Corps
Worldwide

Copyright © 2020 Eldon Katter

Printed in the United States of America by
Peace Corps Writers of Oakland, California.

For more information, contact

peacecorpsworldwide@gmail.com

Peace Corps Writers and the Peace Corps Writers colophon are
trademarks of Peace CorpsWorldwide.org.

ISBN-13: 978-1-935925-99-6

Library of Congress Control Number: 2020910087

First Peace Corps Writers Edition, June 2020

DEDICATION

We are never alone on our journey.
Sometime, somewhere, someone
Becomes embedded in our heart,
Etched in our memory.

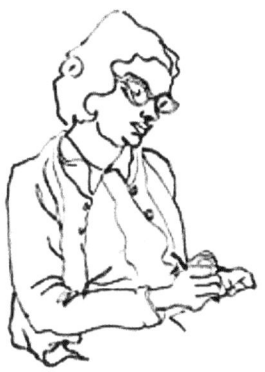

Adrienne: Writing letters home from Uganda.

This book is dedicated to
Adrienne Damon Katter
Peace Corps Volunteer
Wife of 50 plus years
Mother of three
My best friend
My soulmate
True love
Though separated at times by time and distance
True soul mates share a bond that flows
Continually between them.

Memories reveal the core of who we are.

CONTENTS

"Umntu ngumntu ngabantu"

ANCIENT PROVERB IN THE XHOSA LANGUAGE
OF SOUTH AFRICA

Translation:
"A person is a person because of other people"

ACKNOWLEDGMENTS

Invisible Trustees

To trust is to rely on the character of someone — a role model. To trust is to place confidence in someone — a mentor. To trust is to depend on the honesty of someone — a trustee. I believe I've had a host of invisible trustees looking over my shoulder throughout this writing process.

First of all, there is my wife and fellow Peace Corps Volunteer Adrienne Damon Katter. This book would not have been possible without her support and encouragement. She is an editor's editor.

Also trusted confidants of our Peace Corps experience were the guys I lived with in Harar, Ethiopia — Sebsibe, Richard, Kent, Danny, Michael, and John. Each, in his own way, became a role model, a mentor, a trustee. Their invisible voices continue to fuel memories.

Although I did not get to know John Coyne or Marian Haley Beil during Peace Corps training or the two years we served in Ethiopia, they too became trusted influences on the publication of this book. Their efforts on behalf of Peace Corps writers and the founding of Peace Corps Worldwide are remarkable achievements. I especially want to thank Marian for designing and editing this book.

I am blessed to have been surrounded by invisible trustees. Thank you all.

PREFACE

I cannot take myself seriously
As an erudite writer of poetry.
To make such a boast
Would be a claim of utmost
Scholarly dishonesty.
Confused by false praises
I persist in playing with words
With the twist of a sword
Writing with impure blurbs
Using inkhorn terms
Infused with overused phrases.

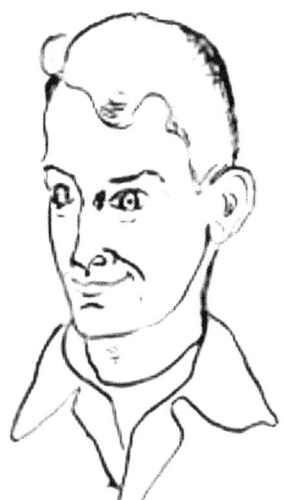

Self-portrait. 1957

PROLOGUE

MEMORY SKETCHES —
A NEW KIND OF TRUTH

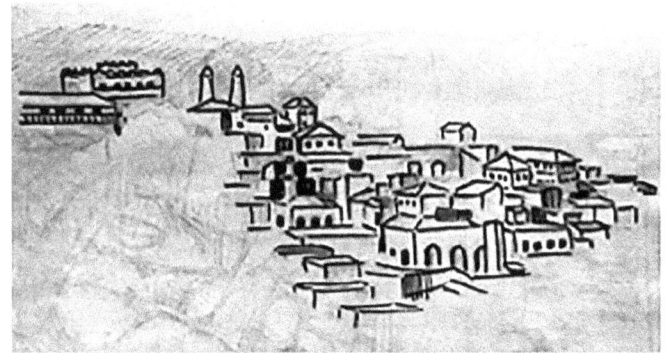

Harar, Ethiopia: An Unfinished Memory

As time passes
Memories are distorted,
Images become less defined,
Ideas more refined
In ebbing light.

A Way of Seeing

Sketching is a way of seeing:
Noticing beauty
Subtleties and patterns
In our surroundings.
Sketches
Like memories
Are silent impressions
Carried away from chance encounters
Randomly bound.
Sketching is a way of remembering:
Collecting evidence of being at a place in
Time
Recording details
Documenting impressions.
Sketching becomes a way of thinking:
Considering the gestalt
Abstracting the essence
Analyzing relationships
Choosing essentials
Sketching is a way of seeing truth
Creating threads of memory.

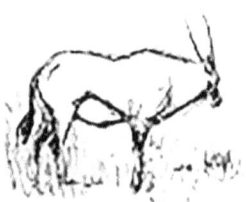

Eland: Free to Roam

Threads of Memory

The
Fabric
Of life is
Shaped by faith
Toned by reason
Honed by curiosity
Lightened by balance
Brightened by reflection.
Delicate and fragile
Though it may be
The fabric of life
Is held together
By threads of
Memory.

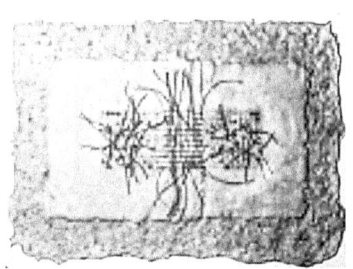

Handmade paper with sisal threads & graphite

The Fine Art of Memory

Memory over time
Becomes an artfully altered
Anthology of stories without chapters
Loose pages without sequence
Anonymous authors
Characters without faces
Unnamed places
Histories without time
Odes and poems without rhyme
Diaries with missing days
Ballets without plies
An echoic chorus of repeated refrains
Lyrical verses about joys and pains
A drama of love, illusion and comedy
Reality, loss and tragedy
Staged and performed each day
In a slightly varied way.

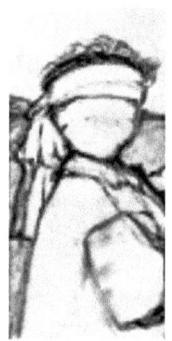

Anonymous

MAKING MARKS —
SKETCHING AND POETRY AS PROCESS

Pen

Pencil

Crayon, brush

Marks made swiftly

In a rush

More deliberate

When there's time

Sometimes with a contour line

Or sweeping gestures unrefined

Sometimes more detailed with stipples

Or lots and lots of tiny dots and ripples

Sometimes capturing shadows and light

Shading with gradations

From black to white

Sketching on the go.

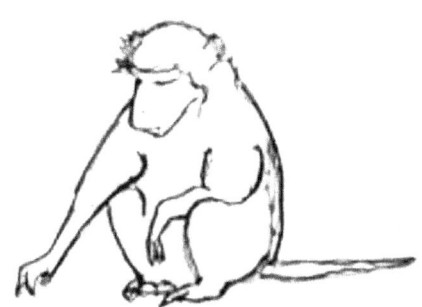

"Marks can be made with fingers, too."

Pen
Pencil
Paper, ink
Jotting in cursive
Sometimes a bit alliterative
Choosing words most expressive
Rendering the beautiful and sublime
Without the burden of obvious rhyme
Forming connections line by line
Layering meaning to refine
Shaping language
Page by page
A process
More or
Less
So

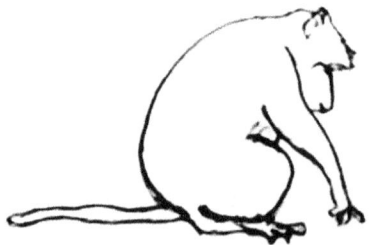

"Love letters in the sand . . .."

MAKING MEANING —
SKETCHING AND POETRY AS NARRATIVE

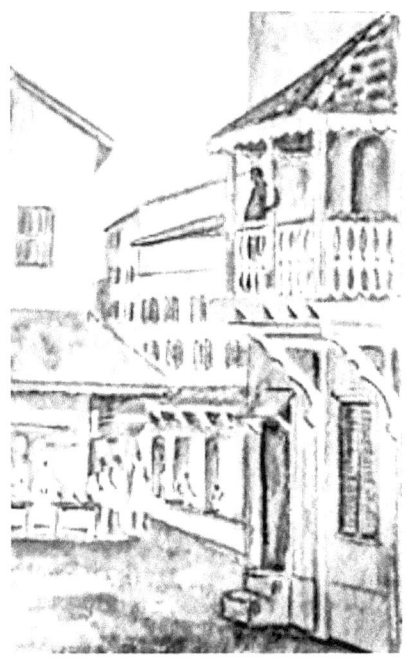

Person of Interest in Zanzibar

We enter the narrative at an angle,
Sorting through a tangle
Of misconceptions and contradictions,
Curating our experiences
Creating a new dimension of
Truth.

We give
New meaning
To once vivid realities.
We enhance the narrative
With poetry, ideas, and images
Scenes sketched on scraps of paper
Ideas scribbled around the edges
Poems written in journal pages
Sensations etched in the mind
All now weathered remnants
Of personal journeys
And global pursuits
Far, far away
From our
Roots.

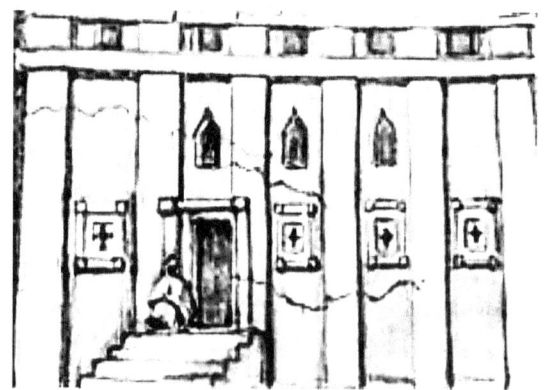

Rock hewn church, Lalibella, Ethiopia

POETRY SKETCHES
A PEACE CORPS MEMOIR

"Your origin is your behavior."

SUDANESE PROVERB

PRELUDE

BEGINNINGS —
A JOURNEY OF IMAGES & IDEAS

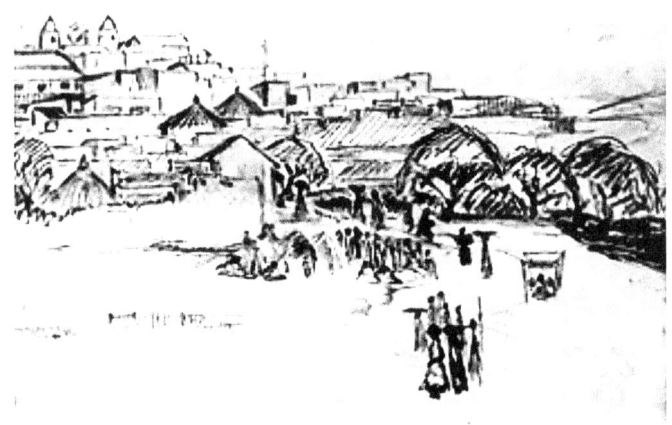

Approaching Harar from the East

With every encounter, enjoy the here and now.
We do not always know where our footsteps will lead.
So, make the most of what matters most:
Today's moments.

Silent Stories, Invisible Lives

In the space of
An uncounted heartbeat
The keeper of forgotten moments
Rushes forward to reveal
The person we are
Not the person we pretend to be.
In the space of that uncounted heartbeat
The silent stories of invisible lives
Become a revelation
Not to torment or torture
But to offer comfort and resolve.

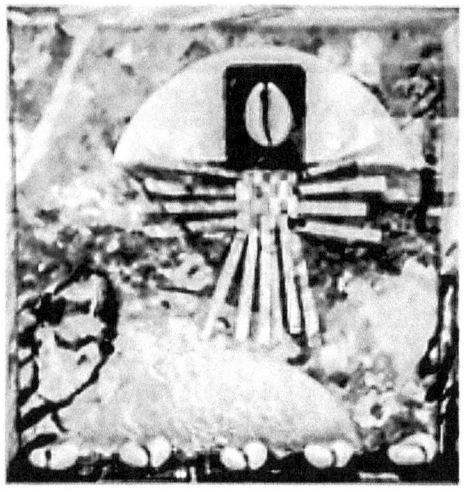

The Keeper of Forgotten Moments
Handmade paper with cowrie shells

Embarking

Every journey is personal
Wandering around wondering
Looking, noticing, searching
Seeking beauty wherever found.
Traveling around, meandering,
To remote places, windswept spaces
To the mountains, to the seas
Sketching memories
Void of sound.

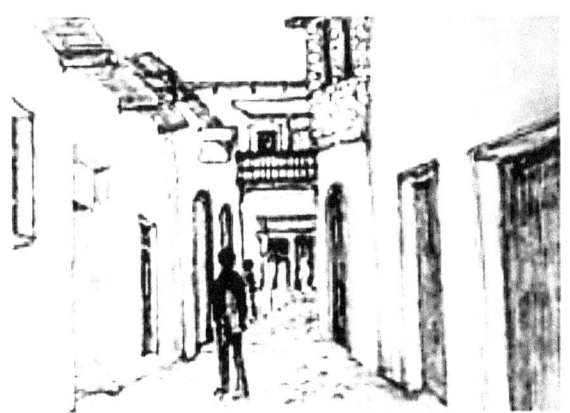

Roaming the Streets of Harar

Embarking on a creative journey takes imagination.
We begin a journey
With eyes wide open
To see new people, places, things
To set a curious mind in motion.
We move forward
With our minds open
To changes a broader world view can bring.
So, with every enlightened notion
A variety of possible solutions spring.
Step by step
Flight upon flight
Choice after choice
We learn by experience
Cultivated with sensitivity.

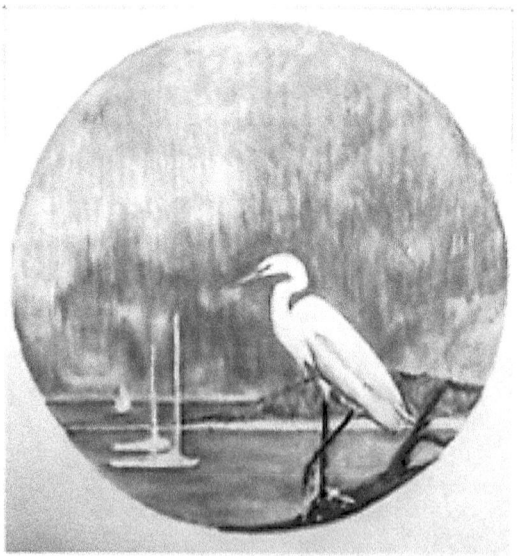

Waiting in the Wings . . .

Sensitivity plus experience builds knowledge.
Knowledge enriches life.
Life fuels dreams.
Dreams refresh memory.
Memory replaces experience
Altered in part by figments of imagination.
If your imagination is out of focus
Your reasoning is not as sharp
As you might think
So always keep
Imagination
In focus.

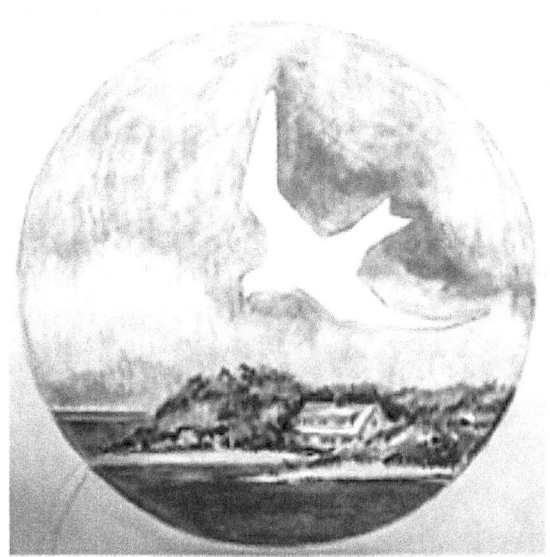

Turn Tern Turn . . .

The pages of a life story
Become filled with passages
Of unresolved challenges
Controversial choices
Ambivalence and
Uncertainty of
Purpose.

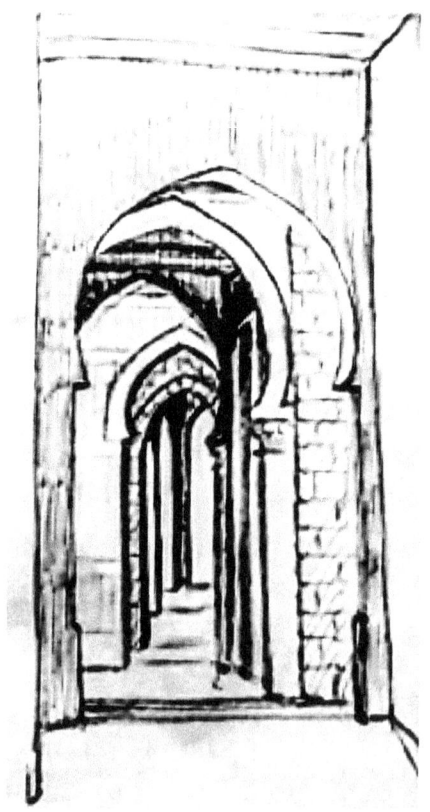

Ottoman Style Arcades, Port of Massawa

Unremembered Beginnings

Our first steps became journeys.
Our first babbles became stories.
Our first marks became pictures.

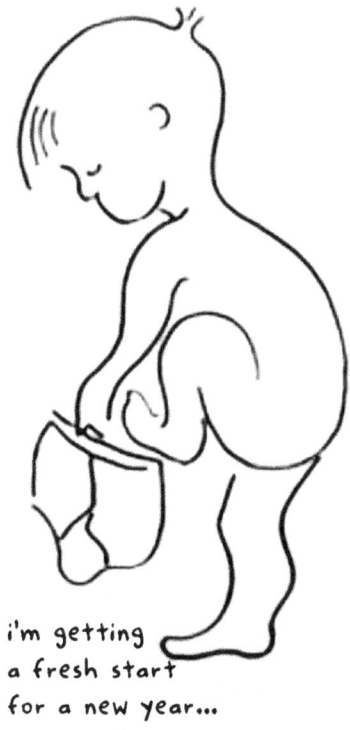

i'm getting
a fresh start
for a new year...

A First Step

Beginning is the most important part . . .

Starting Out from Strong Roots

I am grounded.
So, I sigh
As I watch the eagle soar high.
I am strong.
But turn cowardly yellow
When the Spring rains fall shallow.
I am graceful in the wind.
But I joyfully weep
As the Summer rains seep deep
Into the bank where I stand.
Then suddenly I'm aglow
Feeling my willowy branches dip low
Into the winding creek's flow.
It's then I remember
I am rooted in Hoosier soil.

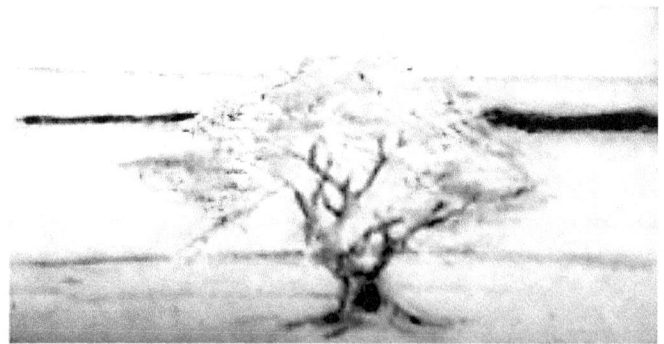

A tree on our farm in Pike County, Indiana

Whoopee Whoopee Wee

At the end of a long day on his Indiana farm
My grandpa would rock in his rocker
And entertain me, peeling apples
With one long, continuous
Unbroken curl of thin
Crisp red skin
And then
He would
Rosin a bow
Pick up his fiddle
Place it under his chin
Turn dark wood keys to tune it
Tap his foot and begin to play a jig for me.
Whoopee, whoopee, wee.
A childhood memory.

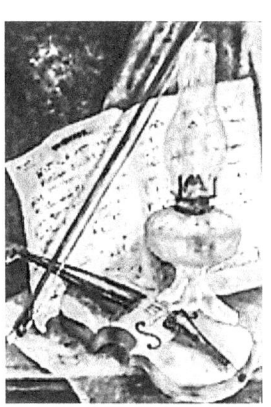

Childhood Memories
Oil on canvas

A Grandfather's Gift

Craft matters.
When you want to —
Plan something efficiently,
Craft matters.
Execute an idea carefully,
Craft matters.
Create something inventively,
Craft matters.
Make something beautifully,
Craft matters.
Actually
When you want to
Do anything that's worth doing at all,
Craft matters.
Or so my grandfather said.
Skilled work is an ideal to strive for.

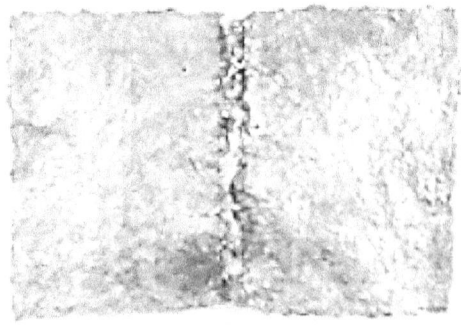

Slight Imperfection
Handmade paper

Craft or Chance

Scissors cut paper
Paper covers rock
Rock breaks scissors
By chance.
But the skill
To craft beauty
Takes ideas
Patience
Practice
Passion
Play
Risk
Joy.

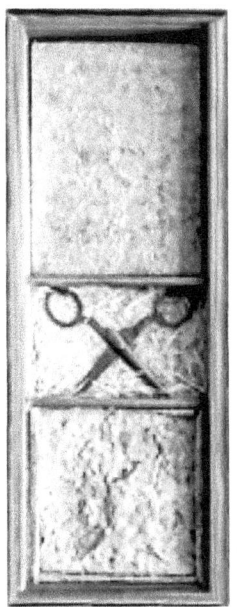

Rock, Scissors, Paper
Handmade paper, travertine, school scissors

Food for Thought

When creating
There are times
To plan a route to follow
There are times to take a path
Not knowing where it may lead
A spark of an idea for this
A spark of an idea for that
Nothing whole
Nothing concrete
Nothing orderly
Nothing complete
Just pieces to process
And actions to assimilate.
It's all food for thought.

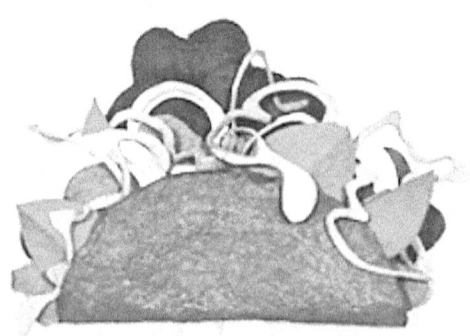

Taco. Series: Food for Thought
Handmade paper

BECOMING & BELONGING:
A PATH TO THE FUTURE UNFOLDS

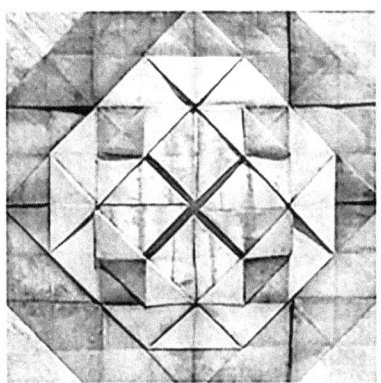

Knowledge Unfolding
Handmade paper origami

Hope gives us confidence
    To trust in our belief that the future we deserve,
        But which is not yet clearly within sight,
            Will continue to unfold and shape
                Our lives.

A Journey of Becoming

All of life is a quest.
A journey of becoming.
An uphill climb to reach
Yet another level
Of personal best;
A trail of challenges
That constantly test
Our endurance to explore
The unending landscape
Of discovery.

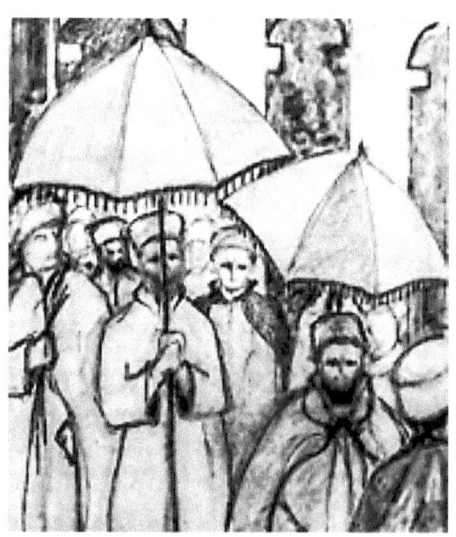

Processional of Ethiopian Orthodox Priests

Becoming an Art Educator

The days of our lives unfold
To reveal a desire for belonging
To a social and professional community,
A desire for personal fulfillment,
And an openness to change.

Searching for meaning and purpose in life
Is the core of what it means to be human.

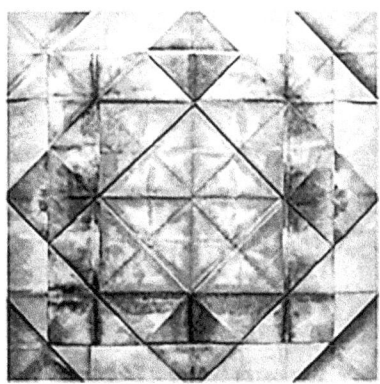

Origami
Handmade, tie-dyed paper.

Acquiring New Skills

The thrill
Of learning a new skill
Exceeds the need to pay a bill
For a skill will last 'til
We are far too ill
To weave a textured twill
To write a trilogy with a quill
To use a drill to set a sill
To sew a fashionable frill
Even then memory of skill
Will still instill
Tranquility

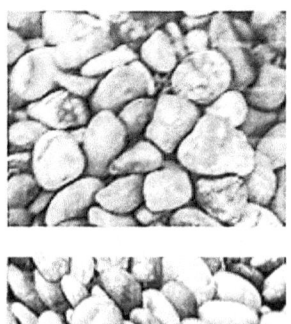
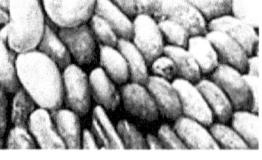

River Rocks
Colored pencil

An Ideal to Strive For

When considering work
Skills are necessary
Soft skills for opening doors
Hard skills for demanding chores
So, a balance would be exemplary

When preparing for work
A pleasant, positive attitude
Facilitates teamwork and cooperation
Responsibility and self-motivation
Garnering praise and gratitude

When starting to work
Steadfastness and dependability
Are important assets
And highly desirable skill sets
As are dedication, diligence and reliability

When busy at work
Character and loyalty
Are oft put to the test
When selecting the best
And valuing one's integrity and honesty
For personal fulfillment

Doing good work will become natural for you
Productivity becomes a goal to pursue
With confidence you will soar
Skilled work is an ideal to strive for

The Creative Process

Engage the process of discovery.
Embrace the challenge of problems.
Explore the many possible solutions.
Expect failures, snags, successes.
Examine results upon reflection.
Extend applications beyond.
Expand new ideas.
Enjoy the electricity
Of the creative process.

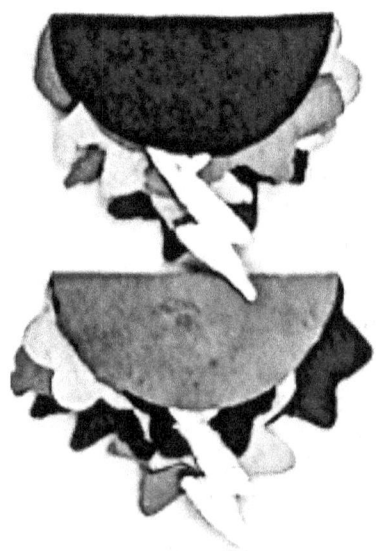

Lightning Bolt Taco
Handmade paper

Vocabulary Test

Knowledge: identification of a problem.
Skill: the ability to perfect a solution.
Attitude: the desire for perfection.
Design: efficient organization.
Work: process of production.
Play: reflective imagination.
Craft: guide to completion.
Art: the total spectrum -
Inception to creation
To final appreciation.

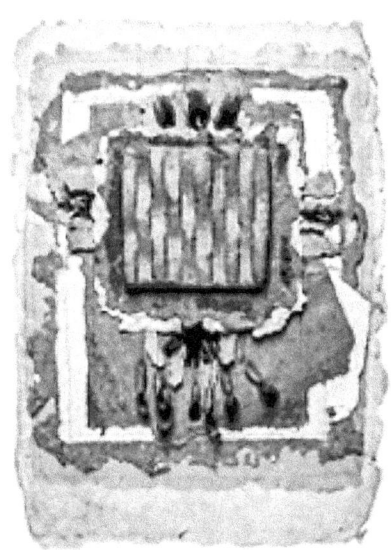

Earth, Wind, Fire, Water.
Handmade paper

On Becoming A Teacher

Teachers,
Counselors, tutors, guides
Coaches, advisors, instructors.
To some they are viewed as mentors.
To others they are viewed more like tormentors.
The difference is trust — mutual trust.
To trust is to rely on the character of someone.
To trust is to place confidence
In the ability of someone.
To trust is to depend on the strength of someone.
To trust is to believe in the trustfulness of someone.
To trust is to have hope in someone.
To trust is to have faith.
Thus, to be a mentor is to be a trusted guide —
A teacher whom we trust and who also trusts us.
To have a mentor is to be in the presence of an invisible
trustee.

The most efficient and effective learning occurs
When student/teacher relationships
Are grounded in trust.

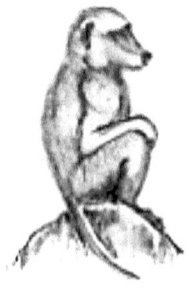

Teaching on Trial

Guilty as charged, your honor,
It started as an idealistic journey.
But no, your honor,
I did not have a three month
Summer vacation at taxpayers' expense.
Yes, your honor,
I admit that I did openly question
The benefits of standardized testing for students
When they received no feedback on their errors.
But no, your honor,
I will never admit to the charge
Of neglecting the basics and wasting students' time
On inquiry and creative problem solving,
Or as you put it, trivial pursuits.
Well, if you put it that way your honor,
I suppose I am guilty of teaching things
Other than the basic core subjects.
After all,
The arts are an essential part of human experience.
They are a means of connecting within
And among communities.

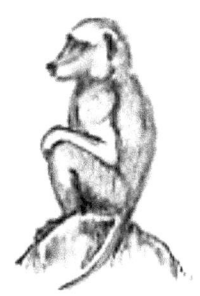

Stories, Marks and Pictures

Once upon a time
In lands far away
People told stories
About their day
Making marks and pictures
In stone and clay . . .
Everywhere, throughout time
Art has been a way
For people to tell stories
About work and play
Simple life from day to day
About forays and glories
Exploring distant territories . . .
So here and now
Where we live today
We can look at art
From places and times far away
And wonder why and how
It still has something important to say
About what it means to be human...
Stories, marks and pictures
Are good places to start understanding
Human experience.

Art & Human Experience

Artists make art.
Viewers make meaning.
Artists draw.
Viewers draw out.
Artists observe and render.
Viewers observe and read into.
Artists create.
Viewers re-create.

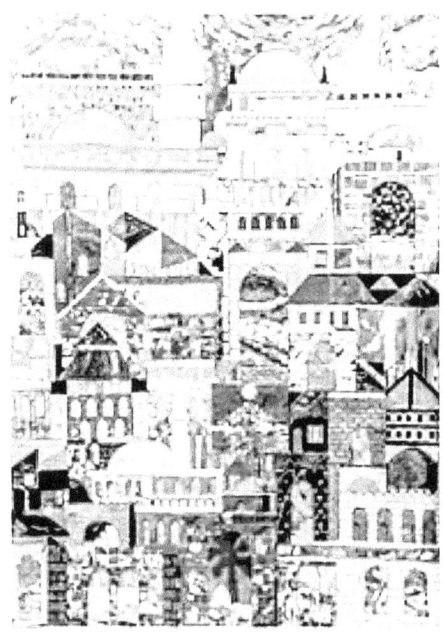

Hometown: Common Ground Found
Handmade paper collage

""Even the longest night has its dawn."

ETHIOPIAN PROVERB

THE PEACE CORPS EXPERIENCE

CONNECTING CULTURES

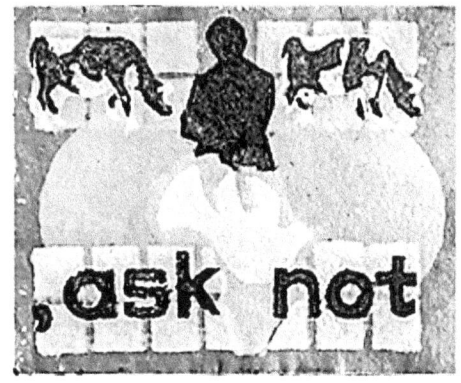

Self-portrait
Handmade paper lamination

We all have a responsibility to ourselves,
But more importantly to the society,
To make the most of opportunities
Available to us — not for us —
But for others.

An Enduring Memory

We answered the inaugural call
"Ask what you can do for your country"
And by the following Fall
Of 1962 we were with the Ministry
Of Education in exotic Harar
Preparing teachers for rural elementary
Schools spread near and far
Throughout the provinces of Ethiopia

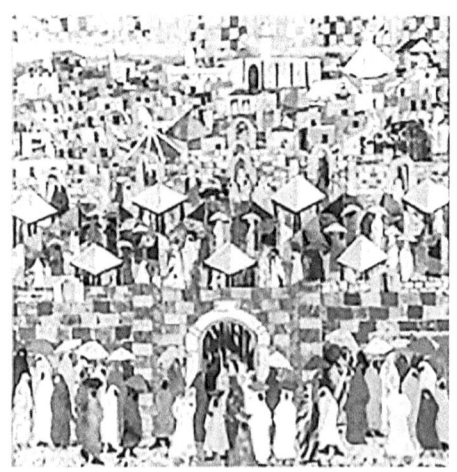

Memory of Harar
Handmade paper collage

Becoming Properly Vetted

The year was 1961.
The Peace Corps was new.
The application process quite long.
So conditional acceptance was early in 1962.
Then came the vetting.
Starting with testing —
A day-long series of sit down
Pencil and paper assessments —
Intelligence verified; personality classified
Sociability diagramed; interests reframed
Language aptitude ascertained
For me, at Loyola University in Chicago.
Meanwhile, I had to provide an accurate list
Of all the places I had lived/studied/worked since birth —
Starting with the first 17 years:
P.O. Box 20. Stendal, Indiana.
Followed by 4 different locations in Evansville, Indiana.
Followed by 1 now forgotten summer address in Indianapolis.
Followed by a street paralleling a railroad track
In Minneapolis, Minnesota.
Followed by 5 different addresses in Park Ridge, Illinois.
FBI agents actually checked out these places
And questioned folks who knew me.
Acceptance never seemed like a sure thing.
There was always doubt:
Am I going to make it?
Will I be selected out?
And there was still
More to come . . .

Then came training —
Eight weeks at Georgetown University:
Learning Amharic as a second language
Learning to teach English as a second language
American, International and Ethiopian studies
Physical fitness, soccer, swimming, lifesaving
Running laps on Georgetown's track
Rope climbing
Push-ups, jump-ups, sit-ups
More testing and finally
An interview with a psychiatrist!
The doubt was still there:
Am I going to make it?
Will they dare?
We did not know for sure
Until the last week of training.
Some people were "de-selected"
For one reason or another.
Some were placed in "limbo"
Awaiting completion of background checks.
But one thing now seems certain:
We were all properly vetted
And vaccinated.

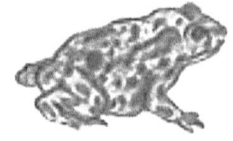

Properly Packed

Wait. What?
A two-year commitment
No mid-tour trip home
Slim chance of phone calls
Letters home best sent
On thin blue paper aerograms.
Wait. What?
Basic needs for two years
Limited to what could be packed in:
One footlocker
(available at Army/Navy Surplus store)
Shipped two weeks prior to departure.
One canvas duffle bag
(available at Army/Navy Surplus store)
Checked in at airport.
One flight bag
(courtesy of Ethiopian Airlines)
Carried on.
Wait. What?
That's all?
Not quite. Also:
Passport, Visa
International Health Card.
And yes, a small suitcase.

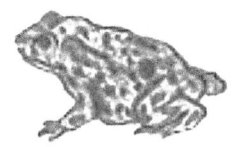

Prepared to Teach

Whether teaching at home or abroad
It's important to know as much as you can
About the students you are teaching.
Where they come from, the languages they speak
Their traditions, their values.
It's important to understand
The people, places, and events that shaped their lives.
So, both before and during your tenure
It's important to make a cultural connection —
To develop a sense of place.

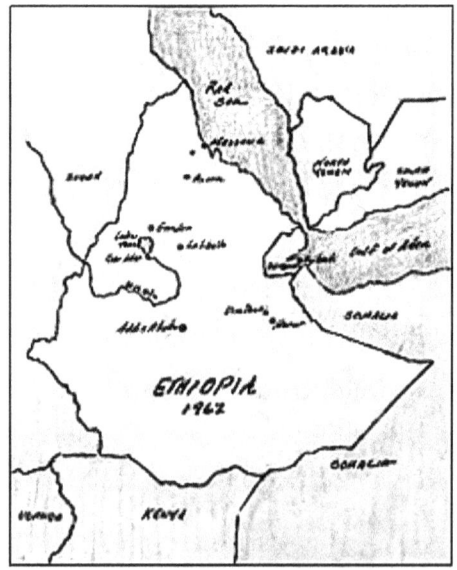

A SENSE OF PLACE — ETHIOPIA

Ethiopia,
Who are you?
Land of origins?
Land of sun-burnt faces?
Land of the Queen of Sheba?
Land of thirteen months of sunshine?
Land of the Conquering Lion of Judah?
Tourism has given you many different labels.
Who, exactly are you? None of the above?
Some of the above? One of the above?
Or maybe, just maybe, all are true.
An always proud, independent
Horn of Africa nation
Never colonized
Briefly occupied
As part of
Italian
North
Africa
1936
–41

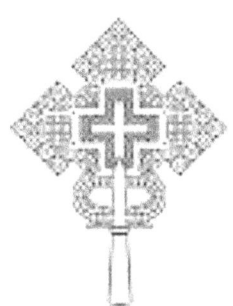

Axum

The Monolithic Stelae of Axum
Solid blocks of granite-like nepheline syenite
Cut from the walls of Wallo area quarries
Shaped into giant monolithic obelisks
Exquisitely carved architectural illusions
Of multi-story buildings
With details of doors and windows
Traces of African, Arabian, Greco-Roman influence
Commemorative stelae
Erected in the ancient Aksumite kingdom
On First to Eighth century burial grounds
Sized proportionally to represent
Degrees of social status and wealth

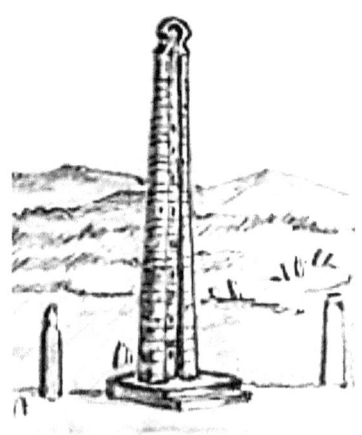

Monolithic Stelae, Axum

Massawa

The Pearl
Of the Red Sea.
Hottest sea port in the world.
Believe it.
A four hour
White knuckle,
One-car train ride
From Asmara at 1800 feet
125 kilometers down the mountain
To Massawa at sea level.
Believe it or not.
The Red Sea harbor is
An intense blue-green basin
Rimmed with mounds of sea-salt
Palm trees, pepper plants and oleander
Shadowy, shaded, Ottoman-style arched arcades
Including the white-washed Mosque of Companions
The oldest mosque on the continent of Africa
Believe it or not.

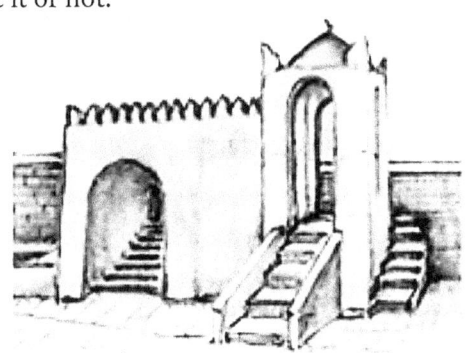

Mosque of Companions, Massawa

Lalibella

In layers
Chip by chip
A solid monolith
Is exposed.
In phases
Chunk by chunk
Doors and windows
Are excised.
In stages
Clump by clump
Interior spaces
Are excavated.
In sequence
Chamber by chamber
Floors, walls and ceilings
Are formed.
In steps
Measure by measure
Coptic sanctuaries
Are created:
The Rock Hewn Churches of Lalibella

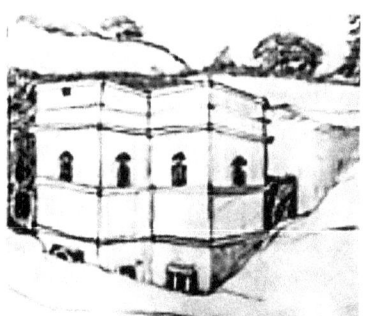

Church of Saint George, Lalibella

Gondar

Once
For centuries
The homeland of Beta Israel
(Ethiopian Jews)
Once
Called the Camelot of Africa
A 17th Century fortress-city
Once
Sectioned into four neighborhoods
Muslims, Christians, Jews,
And the Nobility
Living in the Castles of Gondar
With architectural features reflecting
Aksumite, Nubian and Portuguese influences

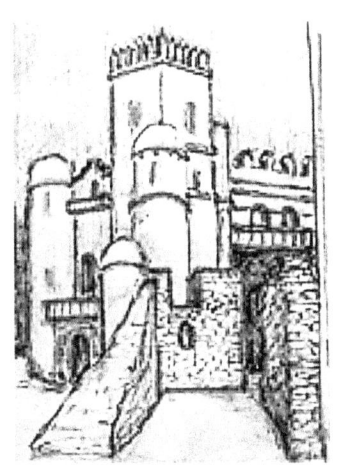

Castle of Emperor Fasilades, Gondar

Addis Ababa

Addis Ababa
Amharic to English translation:
New Flower
Finfinnes
Oromo to English translation:
Natural Spring
Either way, by whatever name
It is the high-altitude capital of Ethiopia
Sometimes called the political capital of Africa
Home to Africa Hall
Headquarters of the United Nations
Economic Commission for Africa
Home to Jubilee Palace
Residence of Emperor Haile Selassie I
Sometimes called King of Kings
Might of the Trinity
The Lion of Judah

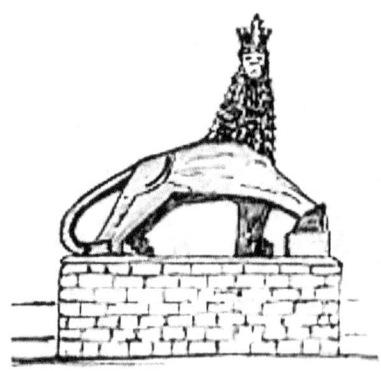

Lion of Judah Monument:
Symbol of kingship, pride, strength, and an African sovereign

Addis Ababa
In early September
Dark, chilly, foggy, damp
A tangled web of intersections
A sprawling explosion of construction
Enveloped in a lingering haze of low clouds
Mixed with the menthol scented smoke
Of dry, seasoned eucalyptus wood
Burning in more than a million
Sheltered compounds.
Addis Ababa
Home to the Merkato
A place that has everything you need
An amazing maze of outdoor market stalls
Connected along unmarked roads and pathways
Some say it's the largest open-air market in Africa
Some say you can get lost in the maze for days
Before you can find your point of entry
Or for that matter, a suitable exit.
There's no easy way out.

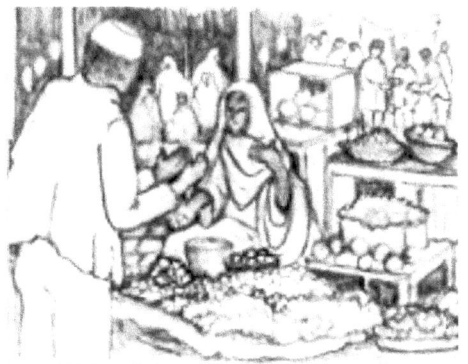

Merkato: No Easy Way Out.

Harar

A gated walled city with high parapets
Cobblestone streets and white minarets
A maze of passageways with musk and myrrh scents
Lyrical sounds and multilingual accents
People of prosper in colorful dresses
People of toil with earth crusted tresses
Street-side vendors in corrugated kiosks
Gold trimmed cathedrals and whitewashed mosques
Muslims and Christians
Working politely together
Praying quietly apart
Open air markets and horse drawn carts
A place graciously open yet intriguingly secretive
A community of talents with much to share and give
A mutual benefit for all concerned
A birthplace for memory
A good place to which to return.

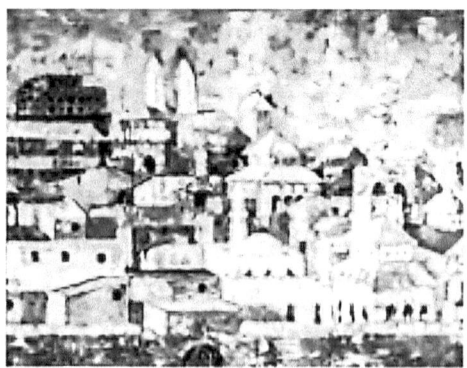

Harar Mosques
Oil on canvas

THE PEACE CORPS YEARS IN HARAR . . .
WITH EXCERPTS FROM LETTERS HOME
TO MOM & DAD, 1962–1964

September 3, 1962

Addis Ababa. We've arrived.

Two hundred seventy Peace Corps Volunteers.

After eight weeks training to teach English as a foreign language, I now learn that I've been assigned to teach art and art education at the Teacher Training School in Harar.

Twenty Volunteers are being sent to the school.

We will double the teaching staff and student enrollment as well.

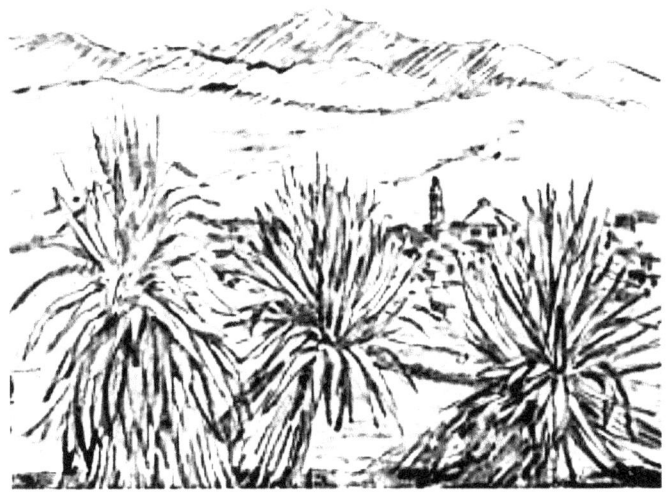

View of Harar from our compound

September 11, 1962

Harar Teacher Training School.

Everything's different.

HTTS is a boarding school for grades ten through twelve.

Student admission is based on high marks on ninth grade exams.

Students come from every Province, representing every language group in the country.

Although Amharic is the official language of Ethiopia, most students speak several languages. All instruction is in English.

Students take education courses along with their academic subjects.

Twelfth grade students do student teaching.

Upon completion, they are given school leaving certificates and are required to teach elementary school for two years before they can be accepted at the University in Addis Ababa.

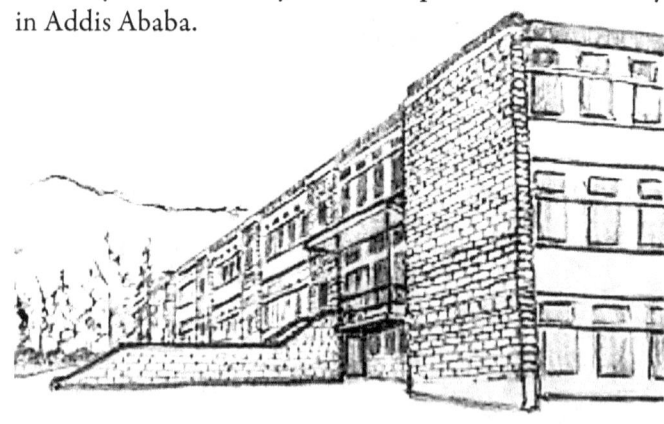

Harar Teacher Training School
by student Tekle H.

October 1, 1962

Art has not been a part of the teacher training school curriculum before. At least not on a regular basis. The school bulletin mentions courses in calligraphy and needlework, but no one recalls that they were ever taught.

I feel ill-prepared to meet the challenge of developing an art curriculum for preparing teachers in a country where school art materials, as we know them, are practically non-existent. This is going to be a far cry from teaching in Park Ridge, Illinois.

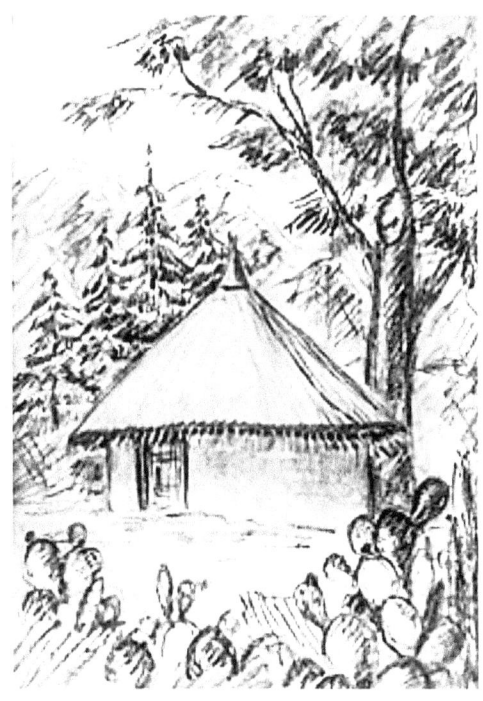

A neighbor's compound

Adjusting

A new home
A new sense of place
A view with few right angles
Few straight lines
A network of tangles
Amazing mazes to unwind
A lost sense of direction
A shock to the mind
A new perspective on space
A new outlook on life
I'm adjusting
I will be fine.

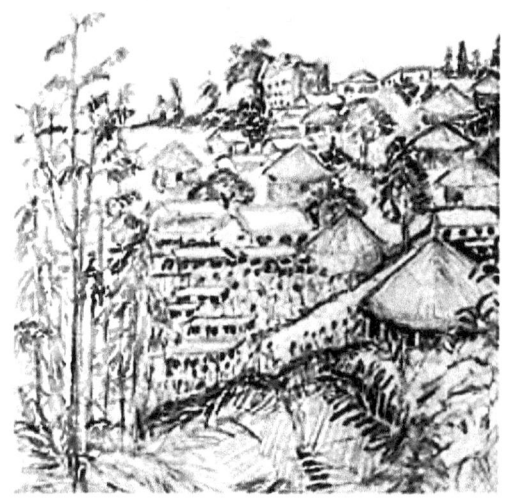

Viewing with a different perspective . . .

October 3, 1962

We have seven guys living in our house. We all teach at HTTS. Six are Peace Corps Volunteers: two math teachers, two science teachers, one music teacher, and me, the art teacher. The seventh is our "host national," who teaches agriculture.

We hardly knew each other during training, but we've organized our household into a productive community employing four people:

- a house manager, (who lives a few compounds away),
- a cook, and his wife who does laundry, (who live on our compound along with the wife's blind mother),
- and a guard (who lives on our compound with his wife and two sons).

Our guard (*zebanya*) puts fresh flowers on our table every morning. He came with the house. He is a cousin of the owner, who is the daughter of the Emperor.

Our house is one of her summer homes. We call it our palace. It sits on about two acres of land on a hillside overlooking the town of Harar and is landscaped with

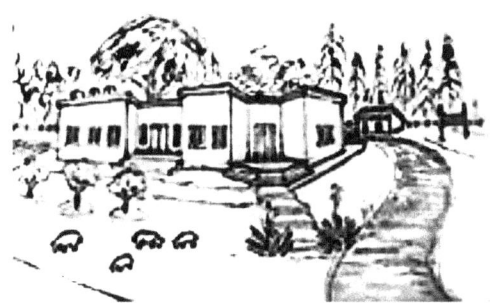

I have a home in Africa . . .

flowers and trees of many varieties: tall slender cedars and eucalyptus surround the property; a small, untended orange grove; poinsettia bushes with flowers 18 inches in diameter; dahlias, marigolds, zinnias, carnations, all in bloom; and a small composted vegetable garden.

We have a large back and front lawn kept trim by several chickens, six donkeys, four sheep, all grazing freely over the property, and an occasional passing herd of cattle.

October 5, 1962

I'm teaching thirty periods a week with two planning periods a day. I have 525 students, all with names I've never heard before.

At the present time, my art supplies consist of 5 reams of brittle newsprint, 24 pencils, 12 rulers, 33 scissors, 1 box of white chalk.

I've ordered materials from the Ministry of Education in Addis, stuff sent by a United States government agency over ten years ago.

Delivery may take several months, so I'm exploring the natural environment and local markets for materials. For now, the students are enjoying a focus on drawing with found materials. I'm taking this material-less opportunity for students to explore their visual world.

I am convinced that my teaching back home was too dependent on, and too dictated by, commercially produced art materials.

Whether at home or abroad, where there's a will to do more, there's a way to do it with less.

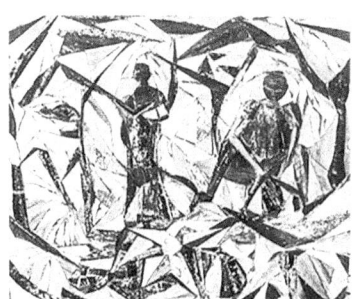

Banana Tree Fiber Collage
Student artwork by Brehanu G.

Connecting with Community

By connecting with communities
Building relationships with co-workers,
Shaping a world view of acceptance, tolerance and equality
Replacing barriers with soft boundaries, open crossings
Common causes, open hearts and open minds
We proceed against all odds.
We all belong to communities,
Participate in groups,
Thrive by compromise.
An organic interdependence
Binds us together.

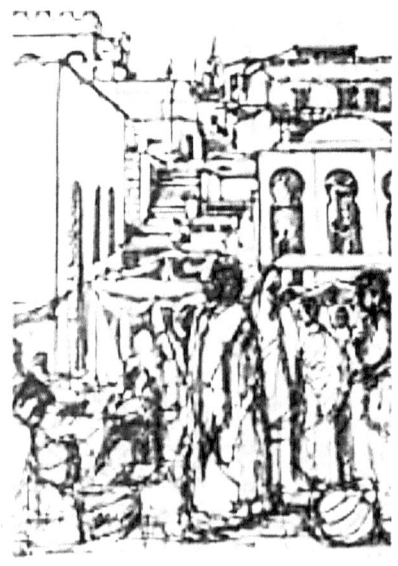

Old City Market, Harar

Art and Community

Art is a record
Of the past, of the present too
Visual evidence
Of human experience
A narrative of who we are and what we do . . .
Art is documentation
Of human growth, of human spirit
Whether it be a world of chaos or one of order
An artist can be the true recorder
Using words, pictures, symbols, creative merit . . .
Art is instructional
A tool for teaching, an inspirational aid
Symbols of cultural traditions, ideals, religious beliefs
Displayed in colored glass or bas-reliefs
Murals, sculptures, amulets carved in jade . . .
Art is a record of our heritage
not to be destroyed but to be preserved . . .
Art is, after all is said and done,
A community connection.

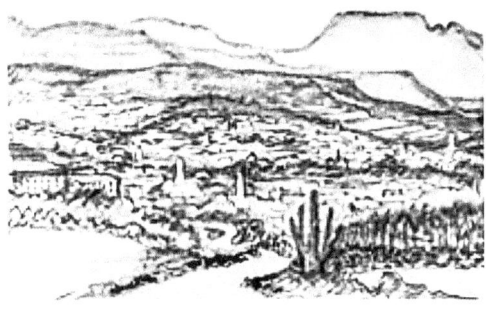

Shortcut: the path to downtown from our house

A Walk around Harar

Walking into Harar
A stone walled maze of narrow streets
Crowded with draped figures
Balancing baskets on covered heads
Beautiful handmade baskets filled with fresh fruit
Or a chicken or two.
Walking around Harar
A place of mystery curled within walls
A sacred center with graves of religious leaders
And stories of sultanates
Doorways of veiled faces
Trying to avoid the gazes
Of a visitor or two.
Walking through Harar
A sprawl of markets and merchants
Chemists, cobblers, tinkers and tailors
Churches, mosques, offices, schools
Coffee houses, restaurants
Hospitals, hotels
And a honey-wine house or two.

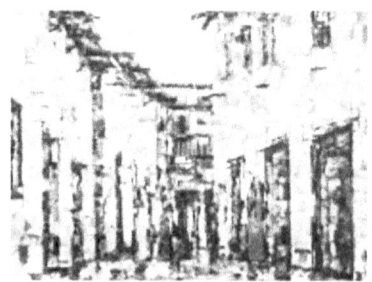

Harar Street
Oil on canvas

Colorful Market Days

Colorful open-air arenas for barter and trade
Orange robed vendors sitting in tented shade
White shawled shoppers buying lentils and *teff**
Red scarfed matrons counting profits and theft
Blue skirted ladies clutching coins in a bag
Yellow dyed cloth hung over poles in a swag
Green cloaked patrons smelling of musk and myrrh
Purple velvet panted matriarchs clutching thick wads of *birr**
Brown wooden bowls full of spices and chickpeas
Black burnished pots for brewing coffee and green teas
Gray shaded donkeys loaded with bundles of wood
Multicolor woven baskets filled with all that is good

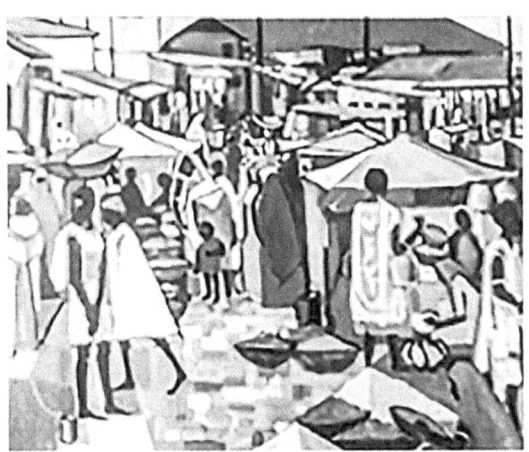

Market Day in Harar
Oil on canvas

---

*teff – a fine grain, similar to millet, used to make flour for injera.
*birr – the monetary unit in Ethiopia.

October 6, 1962

Our cook goes to the market every morning and buys food for the day. We give him the equivalent of U.S. $4.00 from our household account. With this he buys enough food to feed seven guys three meals a day.

Breakfast: eggs, toast, coffee.

Lunch: four courses, starting with a cold plate.

Dinner: five courses, starting with soup.

We made a count of our intake for one day. We had seven different vegetables in addition to meat or fish, and dessert. We usually end each meal with an option of fresh fruit: bananas, mandarin oranges, mangos, papayas, guava, passion fruit, or custard apples.

The growing season here is year-round, so we always have fresh fruit and vegetables. Beef, lamb, chicken, and freshwater fish are available sources of protein.

No pork. No fresh milk. All of our milk is powdered.

We have a cast iron, propane gas stove with an oven. Oh yes, we now have a propane gas powered refrigerator. Electric power outages are too frequent for an electric one.

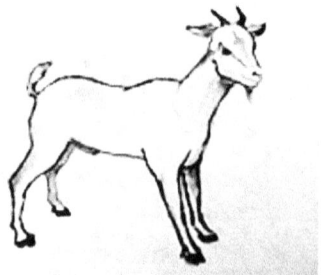

Our resident goat. "I do lawn work, too."

The Book Locker

A footlocker full of books
Delivered to our house included
Selections from St. John's list of
The Great Books:
Homer, Plato, Aristotle
Virgil, Plutarch, Augustine
Chaucer, Shakespeare
Tolstoy, Dostoevsky
Swift, Thoreau
Mark Twain
1984
Catch 22
The Ugly American
Jane Austen, Willa Cather
Virginia Woolf
And more.
Books to read at night.
Books to read on rainy days.
Books to read when there is time.
Books to read for enlightenment.
But so much more can be learned
By sitting at the feet of elders
Listening to their stories
Through translation.
Narratives
Full of double meanings —
Wax in gold.
Wax is the obvious
Gold is the hidden.

Everyone Tells Stories

Everyone tells stories
Written, drawn, sung, spoken, mimed, performed
Some long, monotone, boring
Others short, animated, engaging
Some entertaining, amusing, delightful
Others shocking, alarming, frightful
Educational, informational
Inspirational
Dramatic or comedic
From once upon a time
To then or before
To ever after or evermore
The end

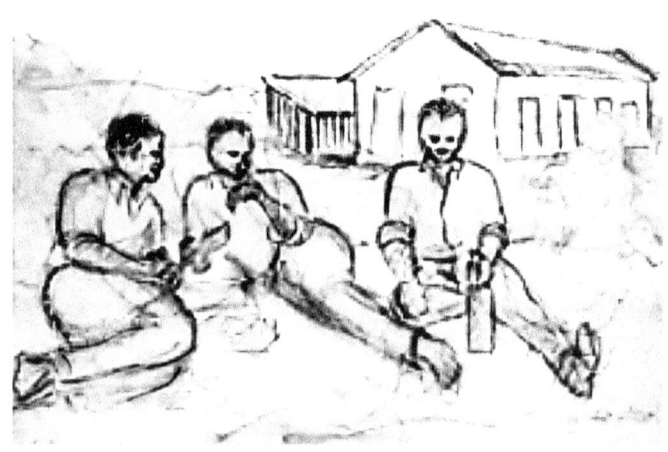

Sharing Stories/Chewing Khat
Tadessa, Sebsibe & Girma

Sharing Narratives

As humans
We are narrators.
We are meant to be curious.
We are meant to be storytellers.
That's how we learn and transform.
In tribal culture, where storytelling is an art form,
Listening, processing and curiosity are the norm.
A storyteller will continue being inventive
And engagingly perform
Day after day, in the shade at high noon
Or while awaiting an approaching storm
Or night after night, in the light of the moon.
For the most curious of lifelong learners
Listening and learning continues to transform
As next happens next, line after line
In rhythm and rhyme
Time after time.

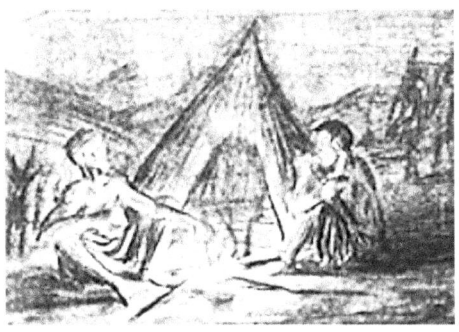

Roasting Corn and Telling Stories
Student Charcoal Drawing by Melesse B.

October 7, 1962

The engraved invitation reads:

By command of His Imperial Majesty
Haile Selassie I
Emperor of Ethiopia
The Minister of the Imperial Court
Has the honor to request the attendance of
Mr. Eldon Katter
To a dinner at the Messerate Palace on
Saturday, October 13, 1962
8 o'clock p.m.
On the occasion of the Graduation
of the 3rd Course of the Haile Selassie 1st Military
Academy
Dress: Civilian, Black Tie.

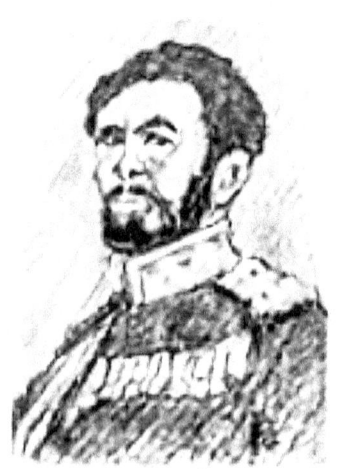

His Imperial Majesty

October 14, 1962

We dressed up in suits and rode our bicycles down the hill to Messerate Palace.

Tables were set on the patio and in the gardens, which were strung with colored lights beneath palms surrounded by tropical flowers.

The emperor sat with the graduating class on the patio. The guests were seated at round tables in the garden. Peace Corps Volunteers were not seated together.

Before we began eating, the Emperor walked around the tables in the garden with his little dogs. As he passed each table the guests stood and bowed.

The dinner lasted three hours.

THE MENU

Tej (honey-wine)

Salad

Buffet, both Ethiopian and European choices

Kitfo (raw meat) with hot pepper condiment

French wine choices

Italian pastries

Citrus fruits

Champaign

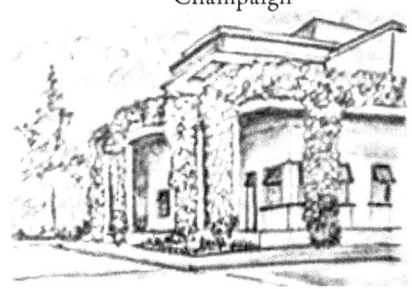

The Emperor's Palace with royal purple bougainvillea climbing up tall portico columns

Politeness

Here
In Harar
When an old man
Or a young boy
Gives you anything
He gives it with both hands
And bows his head
Slowly.
When he accepts anything
He takes it with both hands
And bows his head
Slowly.
Here
In Harar
How do they read me?
Do I seem ill mannered?
Too brash
When I respond
Quickly?
Perhaps people think
I am unappreciative
My actions impolite
If I nod my head
Too quickly.

"The people of Harar . . . show gratitude and fidelity.
It is only . . . being human . . ."

ARTHUR RIMBAUD,
LETTER FROM HARAR, FEBRUARY 1890

When I Am Homesick

Sometimes I wonder
What I am doing here
With flies crawling on my face.
Sometimes I swallow one
When I open my mouth to talk.
I wonder
What I am doing here
With recurrent fever and dysentery
Sometimes too weak to walk.
I wonder
Why I am here
With hyenas as common as dogs
Sneaking into our compound at night
Scavenging for leftover lamb hock.
I wonder
Why I am here
With baboons climbing over our fence
Raiding our garden
Breaking down every cornstalk.
Sometimes, like tonight
In the darkness of this foreign place
I miss the comforts of home
But tomorrow
In the presence of students
I know I will feel I belong.

Hyena

October 15, 1962

Today Emperor Haile Selassie came to dedicate our building.

In my classroom, set up with massive groupings of plants, he observed the students drawing from observation. As he moved around the room, he spoke with the students about their work.

I could not translate everything, but I did hear the Emperor say, "It is good that you are learning to appreciate the beauty of Ethiopia."

Well, I'm sure he knew this was staged for his visit. Under normal conditions we would have been outside.

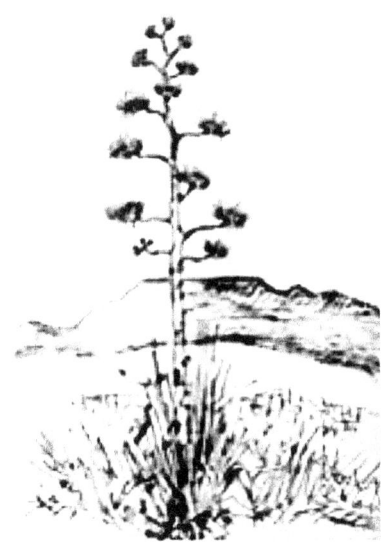

Yucca plant on our compound

"We do not inherit the earth
From our ancestors.
We borrow it from
Our children."

A PROVERB POSTED ON A BULLETIN BOARD IN A CLASSROOM
DURING THE EMPEROR'S VISIT

November 12, 1962

The students have organized an art club.

We're visiting artisans in the area and interviewing them about their design choices and working methods with local materials — cattle horns, sheep hide, porcupine quills, soapstone, banana fiber, sisal, grass and straw.

A Coptic priest, who is an icon painter, showed us how to make egg tempera using pigments available in the outdoor market. He also knew how to make "color sticks," like oil pastels.

An Adari woman, Basket Mary, taught us how to dye sisal with natural colorants and horse urine.

I've also learned that a milky substance extracted from a local cactus makes a good glue, and the chewed ends of a twig from a native shrub makes an adequate paintbrush, but an even better toothbrush.

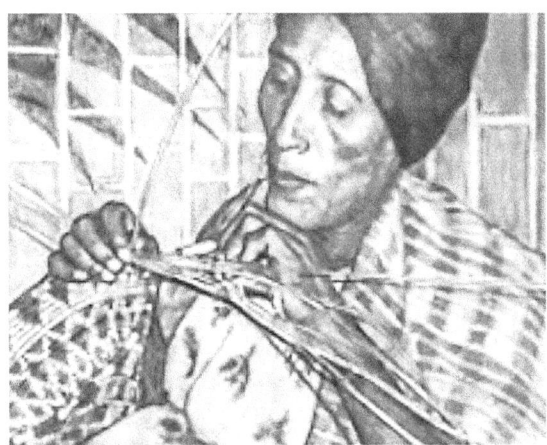

Basketmaker in Harar

About Objects

Every object has a story to tell
Beginning with how it came to be
Ending with how it came to me or thee
It's a story with a chronology
Of the places it has been
Where in the world and when
It's a story with characters
People to whom it mattered
Lives it may have shattered
It's a story with a plot
How people may have used it
How people may have abused it
It's a story that raises questions at the end
Why does it look the way it does now
Did its meaning change and how
It's the story of an object
With meanings that are personal
Meanings that are cultural
And elements that are universal
Every object has a story to tell.

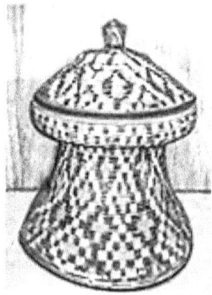

Mesob — a large covered basket used as a table for serving food.

Artists in the Shadow

In the shadow of their products
Individuals make objects with distinctive marks
Thinking and working in personally gratifying ways
Choosing among possibilities, withholding shallow praise
In the shadow of personality
Culture influences the makers
Assigning status, symbols and conditions
Imposing standards, expectations and traditions
Beyond the shadow of cultural mores
World-wide
Makers of objects
Imagine, create and contemplate
Process, express and evaluate

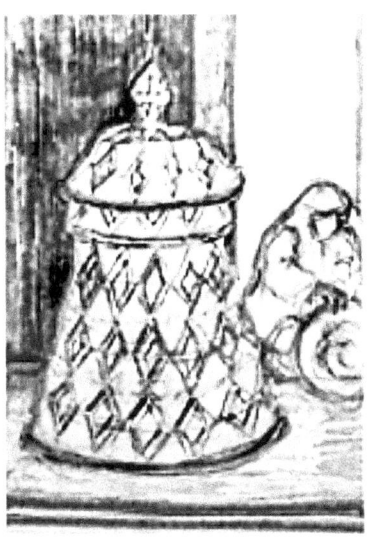

An Artist in the Shadow

"The itch that gives someone skill is not easy to scratch."

AN ETHIOPIAN PROVERB

The Viewer — Looking in the Light

In the light of open minds
Individuals have unique personal perceptions
Capable of reasoning and appreciation
Embracing distancing and interpretation
A key to enlightenment
In the light of group mindedness
Culture shapes and influences viewers
Imposing stereotypes, norms and requirements
Affecting preferences, choice and judgments
Requiring enlightened discernment
In the light of a broadened world view
Human commonalities can be seen and admired
In objects made with technical skill and expressive feeling
That are universally and aesthetically appealing
In the light of open minds

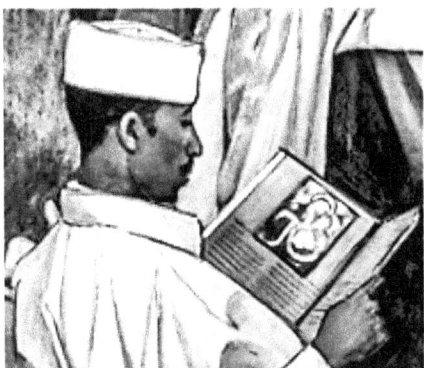

An Enlightened Viewer

"If you want to know the end, look at the beginning."

December 1, 1962

We've been visiting object makers at work in the old city and market. In the process, the students have come up with a set of questions to ask: what's important for us to know, source of ideas and inspirations, materials used, tools required, ways of working, time involved, etc.

During their next vacation, when they go home, I asked them to find someone in their village or community who is a "maker of objects," to interview them, and then "tell their story" when they get back. "How did they come to be doing what they do?" "Why do they do what they do?"

Several things students have already observed about the culture of "object makers" in our local community:

- Artisans who work with gold are highly esteemed, their studio/shops are on "main street;"
- Silversmiths are located outside the city walls, outcasts, said by some to possess the "evil eye;"
- Blacksmiths are also found working outside the city walls;
- Colorful baskets are made by women in almost every household, but baskets of some households are more prized than others;
- Fine cotton cloth is woven only by men;
- But women are responsible for spinning the thread,
- Pottery is a rural village thing, considered to be a less desirable trade;
- Leatherworkers are also found in the outlying villages,
- Woodworkers and carvers are more respected than silversmiths and potters, but less than basket makers and goldsmiths;

- Painted icons and narrative paintings are, for the most part, the work of priests or individuals trained within the Orthodox church.

So, gender, religion, ethnicity, family and tribe are factors in who does what and where. We will continue to discuss the role of art and artists in culture and the implications these long held beliefs have on the teaching of art in Ethiopian schools.

December 10, 1962

We've been here almost four months. Long enough to realize that the task before us is a big one. In two years, we will leave without seeing real results of our work. But I think we are making progress.

After school and on weekends, we are converting an old army barracks into an elementary school that will accommodate 300 new elementary students. A community collaboration . . . all volunteer work. How long will it last after we are gone?

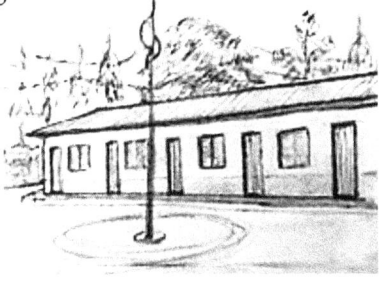

Peace Corps Project in Progress: A New School

Because we have very few books, our students have written and illustrated a 44-page Amharic reader for first graders. Mimeographed copies will be used in our new "Peace Corps School."

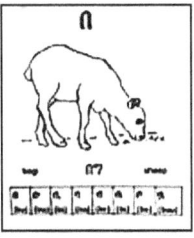

A page in the new reader

December 13, 1962

We do not have a strictly enforced dress code, but for me, khaki trousers are standard. A dress shirt and tie are expected, as are polished shoes (which is hard to manage when you walk two miles on dry, dusty roads). Jacket is optional, so mine hangs on the back of a chair for the day.

Our laundry is done every day: washed, sun-dried, ironed, folded, and put away before we get back home. Shoes are shined before we get up. These duties are not our directives. They reflect the prior training, cultural expectations, and work ethic of our household staff. Their preconceptions of how Americans, especially teachers, are supposed to live, look, and behave have set a very high standard for us to live up to.

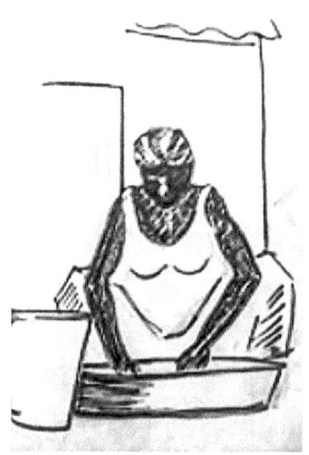

Laundry Day, Every Day
Yeshi

Getting Around Harar

At first
To get from point A to point B
We had two options:
Walk or hire a *"gari"*
(a horse drawn cart with a padded seat).
For the first two weeks
We walked two miles
To and from our school
Two times a day.
Then
We got bicycles.
Eventually
Our corps of Harar Volunteers
Received two blue jeeps.
One for the Volunteers on the hill
The other for those living in the valley.
Each jeep has one designated driver.
The use of the jeeps is restricted
To transportation to and from schools
And one trip a month to Dire Dawa
To buy food and supplies not available in Harar.

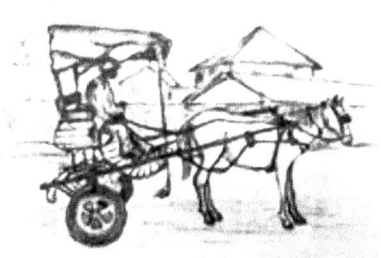

Yohannes, the gari driver waits for a curbside passenger

December 16, 1962

Well, our household has just had a visit from Peace Corps staff.

It seems the Peace Corps office in Washington is prodding the Peace Corps staff in Ethiopia to simplify Volunteer housing. Evaluators from Washington visiting our posts over the past year have decided that some houses occupied by Peace Corps Volunteers are too foreign looking.

(That would be ours, for sure, but . . ..)

They also concluded that housing Volunteers in groups of four or more created a tendency for the Americans to become too isolated from Ethiopians.

(Again, we exceed that occupancy, but . . ..)

The staff wants to discourage American cliques, and encourage more association with Ethiopians. They want us to live in small "Ethiopian-style places," in households of one or two Volunteers.

(Not a bad idea, but . . ..)

Well, here we are, living in the summer home of an Ethiopian princess, with our house being guarded by a cousin of the Emperor. We have an Ethiopian

Werkalemo, our night watchman is on the grounds around the clock, seven days a week, but only on duty from dusk to dawn.

teacher living with us. We employ four Ethiopians and have two families, including two small children, living on our compound. We have even built a latrine for those families.

We pointed out that breaking up our community will be divisive, expensive, wasteful, and disruptive to our work. Now we have to wait for a decision from our Peace Corps/Ethiopia country director.

December 24, 1962

Word came today. We can remain where we are, with a reminder to stay focused on the job we were sent here to do and be sensitive to perceptions of others. This is indeed good news. Our household staff is relieved as well. They have worked with us to build a community up here on the hill overlooking the old city.

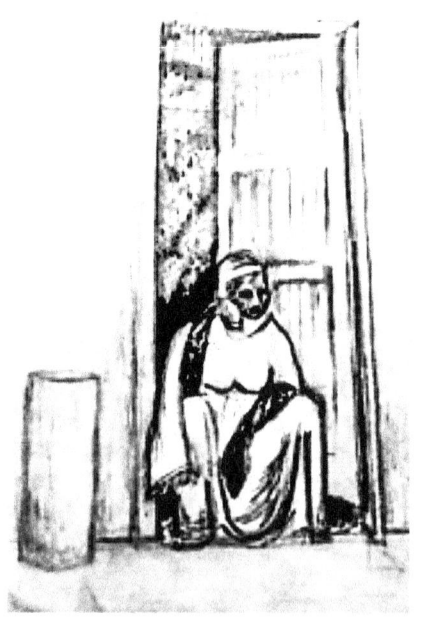

Menna, Yeshi's blind mother, will still have a home with us on the hill.

Christmas Eve

I rode in the back of a Land Rover
Down a dusty road
To a church in the desert
I walked down the candlelit aisle
And sat beside a young boy
His head bowed in prayer
He looked up and smiled
I smiled back
Noticing his big black eyes
Friendly but sad and empty
Then I saw the missing toes
And fingerless hands
He was trying to conceal
I looked away
Hoping he did not see
Pity on my face
He was a leper
Attending midnight mass
At a Jesuit mission church
The service began and I found myself thinking
Of a biblical miracle
One that would not happen here
At the end of the service we sang
Joy to the World
His voice was soft and melodic
He looked up at me
As he sang
With brighter
Happier eyes

December 26, 1962

Sunday the Harar and Dire Dawa PCVs gathered at our house on the hill for a holiday celebration. We played games — football, soccer, badminton — and enjoyed chicken curry and Ethiopian beer.

We had a beautiful tree decorated with red carnations from our garden, small locally-woven, colorful straw baskets, and garlands of popcorn. The base was covered with huge poinsettias, also from our garden.

The biggest event of the day, however, was the announcement of the engagement of two of our Harar Volunteers. Everyone there was surprised. The wedding will be on July 7 at the Jesuit mission church.

So, this new two-person housing arrangement will indeed be welcomed by Peace Corps/Washington and reduce our household by one.

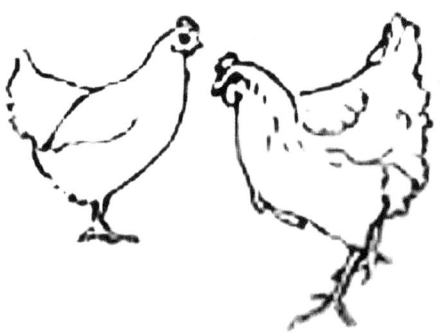

"We survived the chicken curry."
(Chickens on our compound)

Dawn

Sunday morning
The streets in the old city are empty.
Not crowded like yesterday or the day before that.
But it's early.
Things will change.
Tailors and dressmakers never sleep for long.
Soon the treadle machines will appear
On the cobblestones.
Cloth of many colors and patterns
Will hang from the doors and windows.
Money will change hands.
The best man's suit will be made for a song.

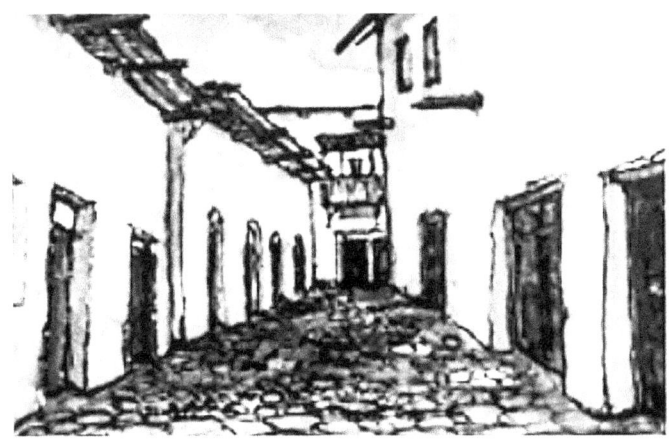

Harar: Early Morning

Second Person

You. (*anche*)
What is your name? (*semish mano*)
You always cover your face.
Why the mystery?
Wait. Don't go.
You. Yes, You.
You've suddenly disappeared
Down the street without a trace
Except for a lingering scent of rosewater.
Yours?
You are the second person to fade
Into the silence of shadows.
Did you know you were being followed?
Were you aware of a second person?
Did you slip secretly through a doorway?
Did you open your door to a stranger?
So, where are you? Who are you?
Really.

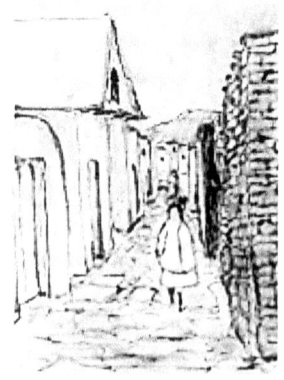

Harar Street

The Medical Kit

Every PCV
Has a Peace Corps Medical Kit
Including an instructional health guide.
Could we survive without it?
Maybe.
But with our household employees
The well-organized metal box is a big hit:
Tweezers, scissors, tape, gauze
Thermometer, ace bandages
Antibiotic, antiseptic, antacid
Iodine tablets, insect repellent
Imodium
Pepto-Bismol
Just your basic first-aid supplies and medicine
Most commonly used for minor injuries
Splinters, cuts, burns, scraped knees
But recently for a little boy's
Infected circumcision
I'd say we've used it
Quite a bit.

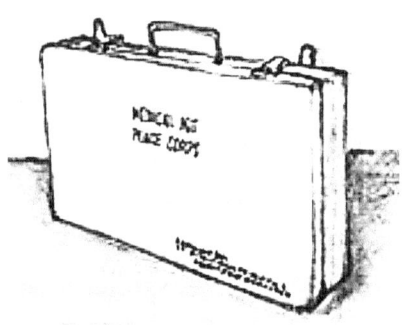

January 13, 1963

We are nearing the end of a two-week break from teaching. I have just returned from a Peace Corps workshop/conference in Asmara, an Italian-developed city, once the capitol of Eritrea, and now the "second city" of Ethiopia. In 1952 Eritrea was federated with Ethiopia, but about a month ago, the Eritrean parliament voted to become a province of Ethiopia. Eritrea borders the Red Sea.

Although the meetings were scheduled for seven days, John, Mary and I decided we had had enough group therapy, so we took off for Massawa, a port on the Red Sea. The one-car train ride from the highland city of Asmara, altitude 7,800 feet, down to the sea level port of Massawa was a breathtaking, fast-heartbeat experience. The track zigzags down the mountains, through 15 tunnels, for 125 kilometers. Total trip time, 4 hours. I was told that a cable car system was used in the 1930s and '40s to carry supplies between the two cities. The buckets could make the trip in 20 minutes.

Our four-day stay in Massawa was idyllic. Each morning we would hire a boatman to row us out to Green Island, a small coral reef about 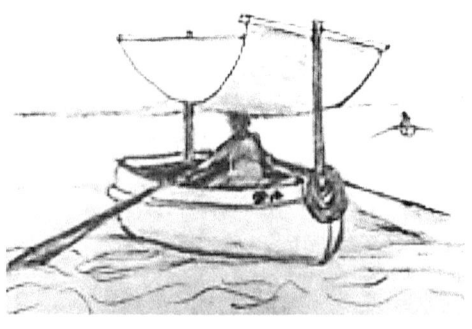 a mile offshore. There we would spend the day. Most of the time we were the only people on the island. We carried cheese, salami, sardines, shrimp and bread with us, as well as wine, beer and fresh water. We would have lunch with our boatman, sitting in the boat under a canvas canopy.

The Red Sea water is clear and very salty. With face masks, we could swim underwater and see beautiful coral and all types of sea life.

I collected shells and coral for my students to draw.

At high tide, as the sun sank behind the mountains, we would row back to shore and have dinner on the roof of our hotel located on a promenade along the harbor. From the balcony of my room, I could watch the antique fishing vessels sail out of the harbor each morning.

Although Massawa is known as the hottest seaport in the world, the temperatures, while we were there, were never above 100 degrees, and there was always a breeze.

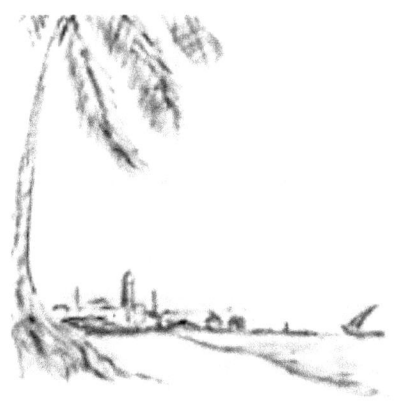

"The one who starts work early is neither hit by the severe heat of the sun nor the burning sand."

AN ETHIOPIAN PROVERB

Massawa Moments

Sunny
Coral island
Sandy beaches
Buoyant, clear azure water
Ethiopia's best kept secret
Green Island, Red Sea
Colorful crustacea
Mid-day tidal pool
Capturing nature's beauty
Momentarily

Sea anemone
Deceptively harmless
Inherently predatory
Meat eating
Flower of the Sea
Water dwelling anemone
Flower-like animal
Predator of the sea
Co-existing
In symbiotic harmony with
Salt-water vagabonds
In search of new dwellings

February 13, 1963

So far, this new year has been a series of unfortunate events.

Event #1 — Sand fly fever.

Fifteen days after returning to Harar after our Red Sea vacation, I was stricken with a high fever accompanied by intense headaches. I could not get out of bed for three days. Every movement was agonizing. I don't wish to go through that again. In that respect, I'm lucky, because once you've had sand fly fever, you are immune to further attacks.

Event #2 — Mysterious disappearance of my camera.

I was with a group of students on a sketching trip to a Muslim cemetery outside the city of Harar. The stonework and tomb structures were of interest. Also, a long camel caravan was approaching. I started snapping pictures of the camels but was angrily called out by one of the drivers, so I apologized and quickly sat down against a low stone wall to help one of the boys with his sketch. I had my camera right beside me, against the wall. When I started to get up a few minutes later, I noticed that my camera was gone, and no one was nearby. It seemed as though the camera had been absorbed by the wall, taken by ghosts in the graveyard. The camel caravan was still passing by, perhaps my camera was now on its way to the Somali border.

Event #3 — Missing backpack.

The loss of the backpack was not a big deal. The tragedy was the loss of its contents. For the past several months, I have been working on an art curriculum for Ethiopian elementary schools. I carried the resources and the only typed copy of the material I had written in this backpack, which traveled with me to school every day. Unfortunately, last week, on my way home from school, I stopped at the Ras Hotel for a Fanta. I was sitting on the front porch, enjoying the conversation around me, the backpack on the floor next to my chair. Again, just like the disappearance of my camera, when I got up to leave, the backpack was gone.

Event #4 — Lost rolls of exposed slide film.

I've been sending the rolls of exposed film to my parents in Indiana to be developed and for safe keeping. Well, I just had a letter from home, informing me that the latest package of six rolls of film, air-mailed four weeks ago, had not been received. I suppose it was a dumb idea in the first place. So now I am without slides and without a camera to take more. Just sketches, poems, and memories.

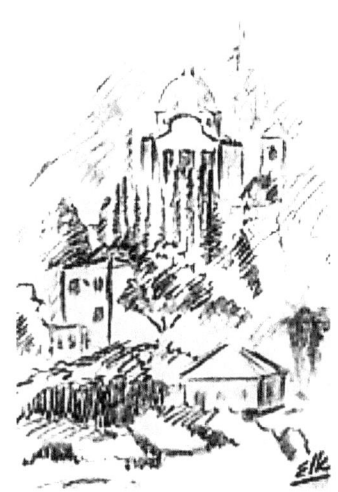

Ras Makonnen Crypt/Tekle Haymanot Church. Harar

"Smooth seas do not make skillful sailors"

AN ETHIOPIAN PROVERB

February 15, 1963

It has not rained since October. During this longer than usual dry season, we pay to have water delivered twice a week by a train of 6 or 8 donkeys, each with two 20-liter petrol cans strapped across its back. The water is strained into a barrel on the ground, then hand-pumped to a barrel on the roof for running water powered by gravity. The water is then filtered, boiled, and rationed.

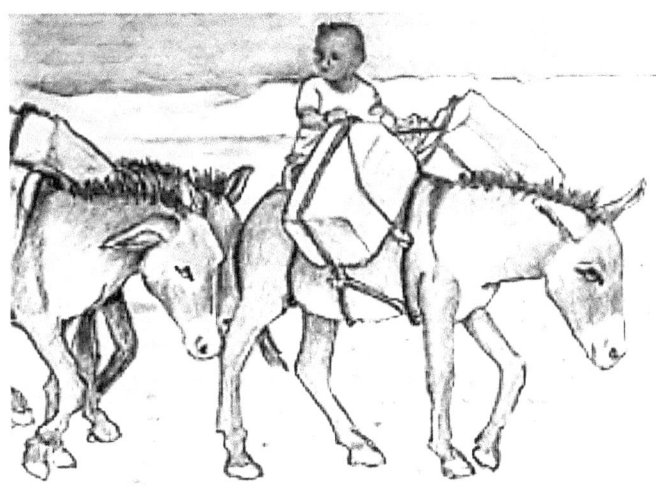

Dry Season Water Main

Small Rains

The small rains came
With the promise of a beautiful garden
Fresh tomatoes, lettuce, cucumbers
Radishes and carrots
Grown in composted soil.
All safe to eat
Without washing in boiled water and Clorox.
But with the rains came army worms
Moving as a solid mass
Under the door
Across the floor
Down the hall
Onto my bed
Over my blanket
Around my head.
Then beautiful moths
Decorating curtains, walls and ceilings
Finally falling
In a flutter to the floor.

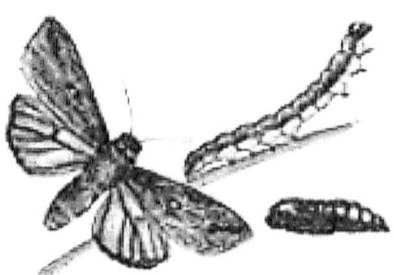

Army Worm & Moth

Big Rains

When the big rains came
The grass flourished.
Our compound became a pasture
For three or four goats, a few ewes
And a small herd of cattle.
But then came locusts,
In massive swarms.
Like a lawn mower
Cutting wide swaths
Across the lawn
Into the garden.
A useless battle.

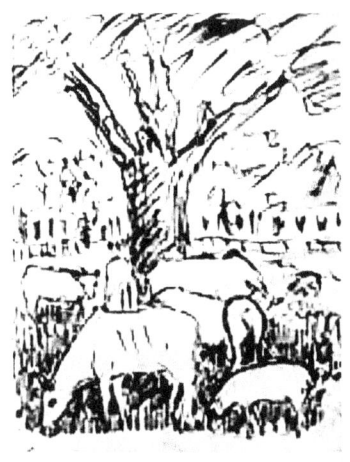

Neighborhood livestock grazing in our compound

Simple Pleasures

I like Ethiopia.
Life here is simple
Quiet, yet full of surprises
Like the almost unnoticed
Graceful pose of a praying mantis
On my typewriter carriage.
A melodic chorus of tree frogs and crickets.
A vibrant poinsettia bush that never stops blooming.

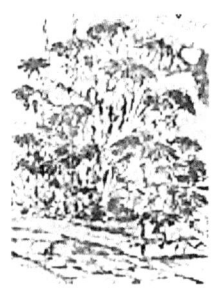

The fragrance of orange blossoms, jasmine, and roses.
A violent sunrise revealing a city of stucco and stone.
The changing hues of a technicolor mountain
Throughout the day.
A shocking orange sunset muted with pinks and purples.
A mountain stream rising rapidly
Through a stone lined gully.
The staccato drumming sound of rain on a tin roof
When the big rains come.
A dark valley without electricity
Illuminated by a lightning storm.
Ultimate simplicity.
Simple pleasures.

Harar after Dark

In the dark of night
Walk to the East Wall to see
The hyena man.
He sits cross legged,
A piece of fresh donkey meat
Hanging from his teeth.
As he leans forward
Two bright amber points of light
Emerge from darkness.

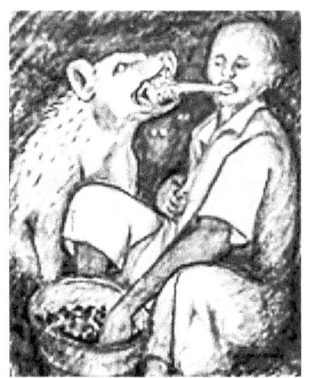

Snap, snap. Just like that
The dark spotted hyena
Takes its evening treat.
One by one they come,
The strong jawed, bristle haired beasts,
To feast on raw meat
Served with daring feats
By one Mohammed Ali,
The hyena man
Of Harar.

March 10, 1963

Gunshots pierced the silence of the night. Screams and shouts from a place down the hill. Then pounding at our door.

Our house manager's 14-year-old sister had been shot by her estranged husband, a soldier. We found her lying in a pool of blood. The husband had fled.

Knowingly in violation of Peace Corps regulations, we put her in our jeep and drove her to the hospital. We took her brother to the Police to report the incident. The husband was arrested in his home village. He remains in prison.

The young woman survives.

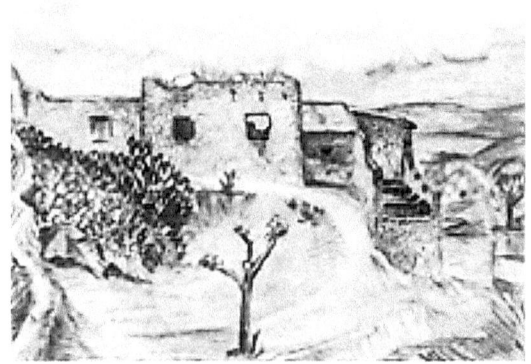

View of Prison Wall on the Outskirts of the Old City

Open Gates

Walls reject. Gates accept.
Entering purports confidence. Exiting portends change.
Leaving behind is hard. Moving ahead is harder.
Walls close minds. Gates open eyes.
Walls crumble over time.
Gates remain open
As entryways
For change.

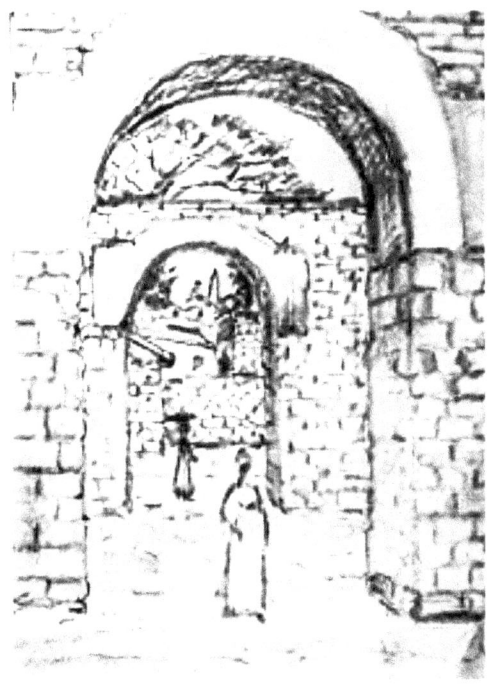

Harar: City of Stone Arches

Surrounded by Stone

Finding my way
In a gated stone-walled city
Walking down cobblestone streets
Through narrow stone alleys
Touching stone walls of houses
Passing under stone arches
Climbing steep stone steps
Admiring stone statues
Picking up stones, kicking stones
Resting on stone benches
Bartering with stone-faced traders
Entering whitewashed stone mosques
Sheltered by stone walls of a highland gated city
Built stone by stone
In the shadow of a stone mountain
A stone sanctuary
A stone shrine
A stone home

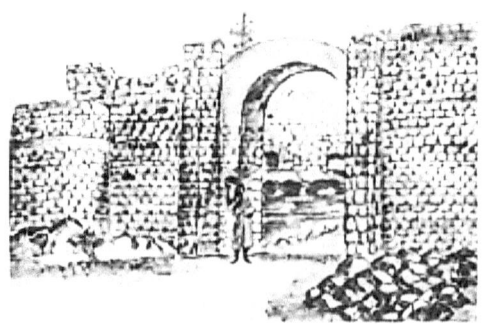

East Gate, Harar

April 16, 1963

Our school has become a showcase for visiting dignitaries.

Our director, Ato Paulos, always brings visitors to the art room because, he says, student achievement is immediately obvious. There is always artwork displayed on bulletin boards, and students are actively engaged.

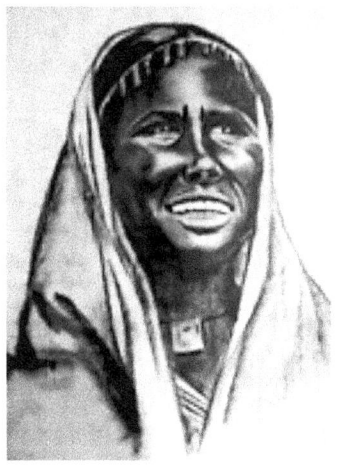

Portrait of a Harari Girl
Charcoal drawing by student Melesse B.

Last week, he walked into the art room, unannounced, with His Excellency Lij Kassa, President of the University of Addis Ababa. His Excellency had some very positive questions about the importance of art education in Ethiopia.

After a rather lengthy conversation, his last question was one I could not answer without pause. He asked me if I would be interested in teaching at the University in Addis after my tenure with the Peace Corps. I was caught off-guard, so I told him to ask me again next year. I explained that I was officially on a leave of absence from a tenured position in the States and was expected to return next September.

Earlier this year, I was surprised by a visit from President Houphuet Boigny of the Republic of Ivory Coast and his wife, one of the ten most beautiful women in the world according to *Life* magazine. They were touring Ethiopia after attending the first African Summit Conference in Addis Ababa. They spent almost an entire period in my art room, chatting with the students about their work and how they felt about having Peace Corps teachers. They also asked me how my experience in Ethiopia compared with teaching in the United States.

May 10, 1963

I was called to Addis Ababa by the Ministry of Education to pick up supplies from the Ministry's warehouse for the summer in-service program we are planning for Ethiopian teachers.

What I expected to be a two-day trip turned out to be one week. Lots of red tape, papers to sign, and long periods of time to sit and wait. The real shock was the amount of educational support materials, all supplied more than ten years ago by the US Point Four program, were now stockpiled in a locked and guarded warehouse: pencils, erasers, crayons, tempera paint, paint brushes, glue, school paste, scissors, rulers, compasses, protractors, alphabet strips, U.S. and world maps, globes, writing tablets, cursive-writing charts, textbooks for every subject and every grade level, workbooks, coloring books, poster board, manila drawing paper, and colored construction paper. The paper was brittle, and the colors were faded.

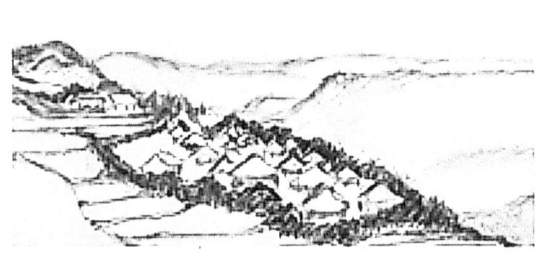

Terraced khat farming in the mountains

And there was more: science lab equipment — beakers, scales, microscopes, etc.; home economics lab equipment: sewing machines, irons, stoves, hot plates, toasters, and other kitchen appliances, all standard electric. Hardly suitable for the Ethiopian power grid.

Daily inventories ensure that nothing ever goes missing. There is no program or budget in place to replace any of these supplies.

Back at the Ministry, I pleaded with officials to release all the materials and equipment for immediate use by teachers and students throughout Ethiopia. I had a piece of the now -brittle colored construction in my hand and crumbled it onto the table, saying "the paper items are just going to waste." I hoped to convince them that materials such as these were meant to be used, not locked away for eternity.

I doubt my words and actions will make a difference, but I did get all the materials I needed for our summer program, and even more for my regular classes and for our two lab schools.

August 10, 1963

Students are now on their long break, so Peace Corps teachers are expected to initiate a "summer project." Since we are a boarding school, the students are away from campus for most of July, August, and September. During this time, the dormitories are vacant.

The Volunteers at TTS decided to conduct an in-service summer program for Ethiopians teaching in primary and elementary schools in the Harar Province, and Ethiopians teaching history, geography, and math in secondary schools in other provinces as well. Peace Corps Volunteers from other parts of Ethiopia were also invited to assist in this project during July and August.

We planned four, two-week long, full-day sessions focusing on methods, curriculum content, and a visual aids "make and take" workshop, which I am now teaching with the assistance of an Ethiopian college graduate who will be with me for the next school year as a "teacher-in-training." He will take over when I leave.

So, we are now mid-way through our summer project, and all is going quite well. All of our supplies came from the Ministry of Education warehouse in Addis Ababa — yardsticks, rulers, compasses, crayons, colored pencils, paper, poster board, scissors, glue, etc.

The teachers attending our workshops are mostly male. In the first two-week session, the majority of primary school teachers were Coptic priests. The elementary and secondary teachers are younger.

We planned very specific "projects" with detailed directions on mimeographed handouts for lettering, including cut-paper letters, which the secondary teachers are very excited about. To date, all participants have gone home with beautifully designed sets of grade appropriate flash cards, multiplication charts, timelines, and maps of Ethiopia and Africa, among other posters. All visual aids projects were related to the content and methods being taught in other workshop sessions.

In addition, each primary teacher went home with a carefully crafted abacus made with solid-color beads and wire found in our local market. I pre-cut the wood pieces for the frame. They had to drill holes for the wire and assemble the frame. This involved a lot of teamwork and trading off of tasks, as some were uneasy about using a hammer or hand drill.

All in all, it has been and continues to be an exciting "summer" project. The Provincial Ministry of Education officials, who have been around observing, seem very pleased.

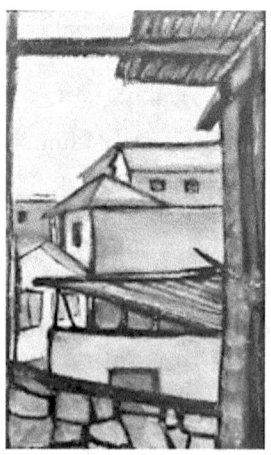

Sticks, Stones, and Structures:
A view from poet Arthur Rimbaud's house in Harar

"To sleep in the midst of wealth is impossible."

ARTHUR RIMBAUD (A SEASON IN HELL, 1873)

August 17, 1963

Before our summer school was completed, our director announced his resignation and acceptance of a new position as Dean of Students at the University College in Addis. With that announcement came the assignment of administrative duties to a committee consisting of five of the Peace Corps teachers — B&B, two retired education professors from a college in California, a guidance counselor, a music teacher, and myself. Our responsibilities included scheduling and timetables for the next school year, staffing assignments, and hiring two new teachers.

We worked well into the night for two weeks and finished all the scheduling and filled the two vacancies before our scheduled vacation.

A new director was named, yesterday, two days before four of us will be flying to Nairobi.

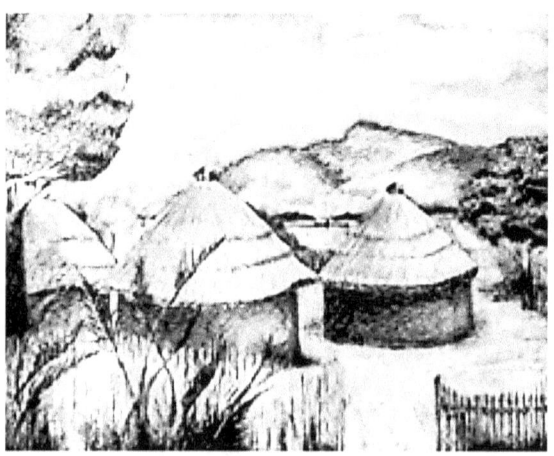

A family compound in western Kenya

September 22, 1963

We had to get Peace Corps approval/permission to leave Ethiopia for our four-week vacation (August 19 - September 19). We submitted our itinerary, justifying our travel as an educational mission and not a pleasure trip.

Our basic plan was to visit places described by Burton, Speek, Stanley and Livingston, all explorers of Africa. We listed *The White Nile* by Alan Moorehead as essential reading before the trip, and also *The Blue Nile* and *No Room in the Ark* as recommended reading along with *The Flame Trees of Thika* by Elspeth Huxley, *Out of Africa* by Karen Blixen, *Uhuru* by Robert Ruark, *Green Hills of Africa* and *The Snows of Kilimanjaro* by Ernest Hemingway, and *Facing Mount Kenya* by Jomo Kenyatta.

Our itinerary took us from Harar to Addis and then to Tanganyika, Zanzibar, and Kenya, where we rented a car and drove to Uganda.

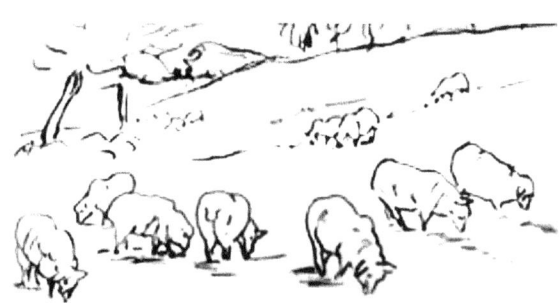

A perfect spot for a picnic lunch in the Kenya highlands

We visited elementary, secondary, and teacher training schools in every country. In Uganda, quite by accident, we met the Secretary of the Uganda Teachers Association, who expressed great interest in having Peace Corps Volunteers in Uganda. He offered to be our tour guide around Kampala for three days, taking us to places of educational interest, all the while pressing us about our Peace Corps experience. We all realized we needed to be good representatives.

October 10, 1963

Before the end of last school year, the students in the Art Club wanted to learn how to make Ethiopian musical instruments. I told them I had no idea about how to make a musical instrument, but I would do my best to help them, if we could first determine what kind of tools and materials we would need.

So, their assignment while on break was to find out all they could about the making of musical instruments in their regions. I wanted to know what instruments would be the easiest to make, the materials we would need to locate, and what additional tools I would have to purchase. We were going to rely on students who had knowledge of a particular "tribal" instrument to teach others.

Well, we now have students making drums, string instruments, simple reed flutes, whistles, and rattles. It is turning out to be a great cultural exchange.

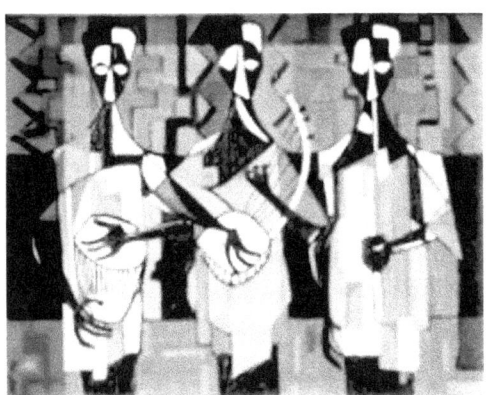

Three Musicians
Oil on canvas

November 1963

November 23. Three AM.

I'm awakened by the sound of a car pulling into our driveway.

Doors slamming. I jump out of bed. Creep down the hall. Kent enters the front door: "President Kennedy has been assassinated!"

Me: "Is this some kind of sick joke? It's the middle of the night!"

"It's not a joke. He was shot through the head."

Me: "When? Where? Why?"

Kent turns on the radio. BBC comes in clearly. The whole household is now awake., listening.

"We repeat. The President of the United States was killed today in Dallas, Texas . . .."

We sat in stunned silence.

Sleep did not come easy.

We were awakened shortly after daybreak by a knock at the door.

Our school director came to pay his respects and to inform us that the Emperor was going to the United States and would not be coming to Harar. He wanted us to notify the other Peace Corps Volunteers.

We drove around town. Most people were still asleep. We faced 40 faces of shock and disbelief.

I walked home, aware of the glances and bowed heads of passersby.

I met two students and greeted them with the usual "*Tenaystillin*," and a forced smile.

They responded with sad eyes.

Me: "The news is very bad today."

The two young men broke into tears.

"We're very sorry, sir. It is a terrible thing. Wonderful." they sob.

Me: "Yes, it is indeed a mystery."

Ethiopian friends came to our house and quietly wept.

Their expressions of sympathy were sincere and touched with emotion: "He was truly a friend of Africa."

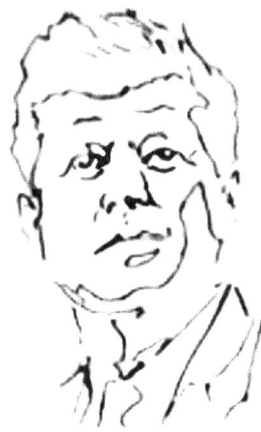

We planned a memorial service at our school for the following Monday.

By order of the governor, all government offices were closed.

Ethiopia joined the United States in the period of mourning.

People in the community joined our students. A priest from the Leprosarium gave s short prayer and homily as part of the otherwise lay memorial planned by Peace Corps Volunteers.

A few days later:

A merchant in town thanked us for having an open service: "Someday my grandchildren will read about the assassination of President Kennedy in a history book, just as I read about Lincoln. Both were great men. And I can tell my grandchildren that I attended a memorial service for the greatest of all American presidents."

The week has gone by. The Emperor returned from Kennedy's funeral in the States and came directly to Harar to confer degrees upon the Military Academy graduates.

December 15, 1963

The Orthodox Ethiopians are in the middle of a 40 day fast, so there is no meat or eggs in the Christian market, and our cook refuses to buy, or cook, meat from the Muslim market. (He once refused to cook pork chops given to us by the US Army Military Assistant Group stationed here.) However, he is OK with cooking the chickens he is raising on our compound. He will, on occasion, swallow his pride and go to the Italian deli for meat products. We can also get fish from Lake Alamaya.

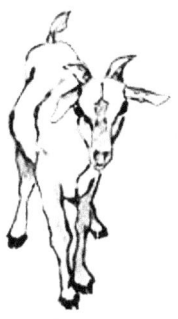

Last week, our cook bought another goat, which is now rummaging around our compound and fighting with the dog. When the fast is over in January, he plans to butcher the goat and have a roasted feast for everyone living and working here.

January 15, 1964

Since our school is closed for "winter" break for three weeks
in January, several of us from Harar hired a tour guide
and traveled by a minibus for two weeks around Ethiopia,
through the Simian Mountains, visiting mostly historical
sites: Gondar, Lake Tana, Blue Nile Falls, and Axum. It was
a very relaxing and unhurried trip, with roadside picnic
lunches, comfortable accommodations, and good food. I
even found time for sketching at almost every stop and, of
course, to write a poem or two.

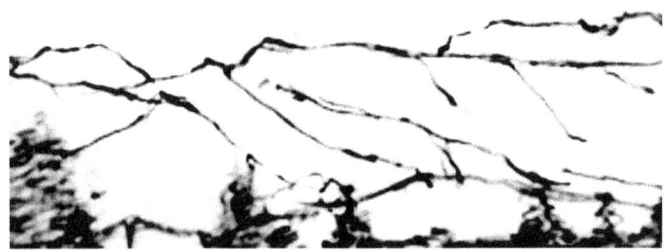

Nature speaks
In muffled voice
Through rugged peaks
Of a Simian mountain landscape
The distant mountains rise high
Beyond the low expanse
Of the Rift Valley's
Deep floor

Bahir Dar

Lake Tana
Ethiopia's largest body of water
Its only outflow being the source of the Blue Nile
Once explored by the Portuguese
Lake Tana
Spotted with isolated island monasteries
Housing libraries of religious relics
And illuminated liturgical scripts in Semitic Geez
Lake Tana
Rimmed with papyrus
The source of reeds for *tankwas*
Rowed by fisherman with graceful ease

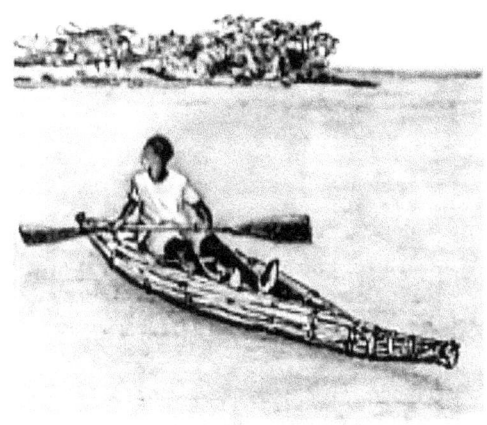

Tankwa on Lake Tana
Bahir Dar

Blue Nile Falls

Beyond Lake Tana
Its sacred source
The Blue Nile river water
Falls with a diapason of churning sounds
Deep into the Blue Nile Gorge
On an eventual northward meandering
Muddy flow
To join its clearer, sister water
The White Nile
Together creating
The Great White Nile
Far, far, far
Beyond Lake Tana

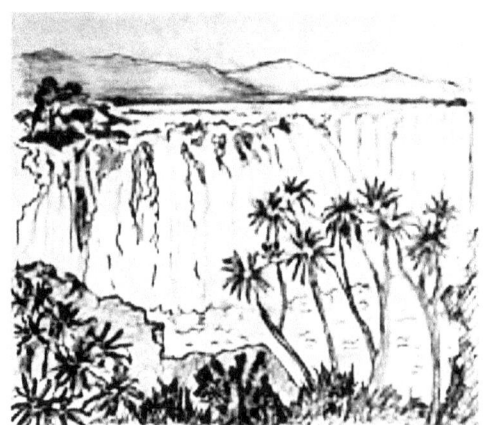

Blue Nile Falls

January 25, 1964

While in Addis Ababa for a few days for long overdue dental work before our vacation ended, I visited the home and studio of Ethiopian artist, Afework Tekle. His home was comfortably modern, his studio spacious and meticulous. He was working on a huge portrait of President Nkrumah of Ghana. We talked at length about his art and art in general. Later, he drove me back to my hotel in a sleek Jaguar convertible.

One hour later I was picked up for dinner by a friend retired from the Ethiopian Army. He drove a shiny black Mercedes. Twenty miles out into the countryside, we passed a man tilling the soil with a digging stick. Ethiopia is indeed a country of stark contrasts on so many levels.

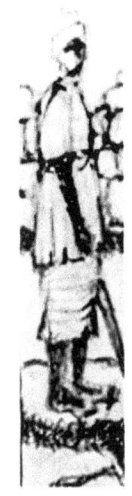

Farmer with digging stick

Islands of Progress

Here we are
Educating our students
To become skilled contributors
To Ethiopia in 20th century days
Spreading islands of progress
In an ocean of traditional ways.
We listen
We hear
We look
We see
Here we are
Educating ourselves
To become better volunteers
In service to America in 20th century days
Spreading islands of understanding
In an ocean of prejudicial ways.
Here we are
Sensitive
To the good that needs doing
Sensitive
To the harm we might be doing
Spreading islands of progress.

Soccer Sunday
Peace Corps vs. Ethiopia

At Day's End

At day's end
The farm lad stops
To take in
The beauty of
An open field
Tilled and lying fallow
In the rain
Waiting
For tomorrow's planting
And the start of new life
For yet another season.

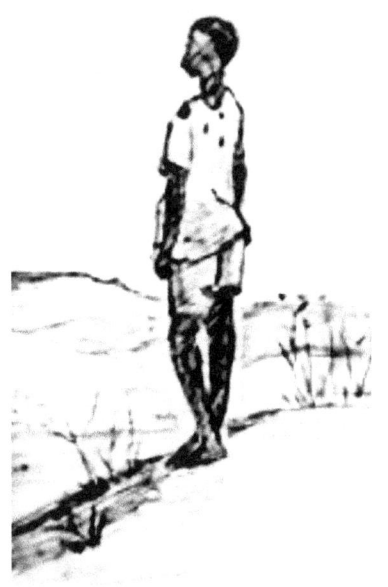

Farmer

February 13, 1964

About our water system —

Along the side of our house, we have four barrels on the ground that are filled once a day by the town water supply. Then this water is pumped by hand to four barrels on the roof, providing us with running water for about four days. That's one barrel a day for the fourteen people living on our compound.

Our hot water system — a barrel lying across an outdoor brick oven — is hardly worth the time and effort to heat up daily. So hot water is taken from a pot on the kitchen stove.

No showers. Few baths. Just a soapy basin.

As for flushing the toilet, the rule of the house is: if it's yellow let it mellow, if it's brown, flush it down.

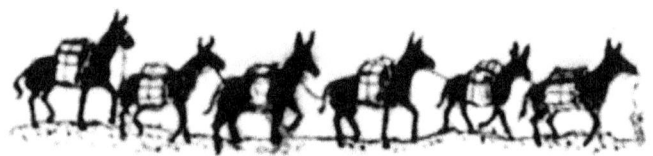

Water Train

Shortly after we moved into our house, we built a sheltered and safe pit latrine (Long Drop) for the household staff we employ. No flushing required.

How to Build a Long Drop

A basic pit latrine:
A hole in the ground
10 feet deep
3 feet across
A floor with a small hole
No larger than 9 inches
(to prevent a small child from falling in
A lid to cover the hole when not in use
To prevent flies from getting in
A secluded, sheltered
Sanitary facility.
No flushing
Required.

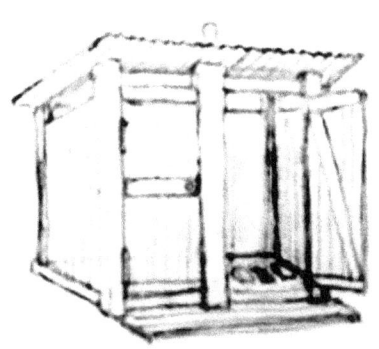

"Who knocks on the door gets an answer."

AN ETHIOPIAN PROVERB

February 27, 1964

They Call Me Kotu
Every time I pick up a garden shovel, they call me Kotu.
Every time I pick up a hoe, they laugh and call me Kotu.
Because I do manual labor, I am called Kotu.
I am Kotu because I do not mind getting my hands dirty.

To explain:
Ethiopia has a very diverse population with more than 80 different ethnic groups. One of these groups in the rural, eastern region of Ethiopia is the Kotu. Kotu are, for the most part, farmers, tillers of the soil, living off the land. When we needed to have a pit dug for a latrine, we hired Kotu. They even helped with the construction of the shed. They are good, hard workers.

I like to think that when the Ethiopians working for us call me Kotu, they are paying me a compliment, that I am a good, hard worker. But I also think that they don't expect to see an educated professional person doing hard, physical work. I hope their laughter is more of a surprise reaction.

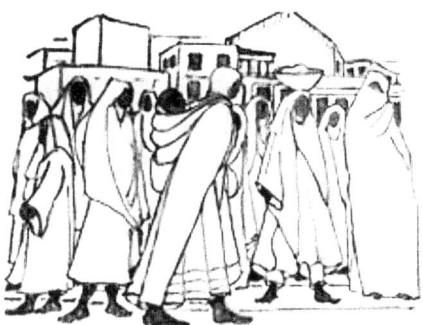

Crowded Street of Diversity

Speaking of different ethnic groups, our students at the Teacher Training School reflect that diversity because they come from 14 different provinces. So English is the one language they all have in common. Although all of our students are fluent in English, they are also conversant in Amharic and have some understanding of at least two or more other languages: Harari/Adari, Galla, Danakil, Gurage, Sidamo, Tigrayan, Somali, and more. French, Italian, and Swedish are also familiar languages for some of the students. I'm impressed by their aptitude for languages.

However, one of my students told me that initially he had a very hard time adjusting to the accents of the Peace Corps teachers: Arkansas, Texas, Massachusetts, New York, New Jersey, Indiana, Illinois, Ohio, Kansas, D.C., Maryland, Idaho, and California. He said we all sounded very different. Our students also had to adjust to the English accents of teachers from England, India, Netherlands, France, and of course, Ethiopia.

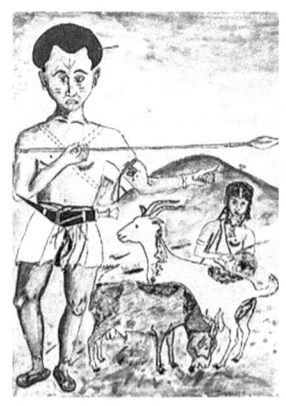

I Am Danakil
Student artwork by Jemma W.

March 3, 1964

Household Changes and Cures —
When we first arrived in Harar, there were actually eight guys assigned to our big house on the hill. That soon changed. The first to leave was our history teacher who moved out after two weeks to share a house with another Volunteer. (He left Ethiopia without saying goodbye to anyone two months later. Reason unknown.)

We were then seven guys on the hill for the remainder of the school year. At the end of the first year, our Ethiopian colleague, the agriculture teacher, relocated to Addis Ababa. Then we were six guys. One month later, our chemistry teacher got married and moved a few houses away. Now we are five.

Each time someone left, our monthly contribution to the household fund increased, and the food expenses decreased, but not by much. Our cost of living allowance can barely keep our household running smoothly.

Sadly, we did have a bit of relief in terms of employee outlay. The cook's wife, who did our laundry recently left, not of our doing, but of her husband's. Right in our backyard, he divorced her, saying "I divorce you" three times. So, our laundress and her blind mother were sent away that very day. The back story here is that she had not only been unfaithful, but she contacted syphilis and, in turn, infected him. So, we made sure that both the cook and his wandering wife received medical attention for a penicillin cure.

April 10, 1964

One thing I never mentioned before: our staff has Saturday afternoons and Sundays off. Our cook comes in on Sunday evening and prepares a simple pasta supper for us: spaghetti with meat sauce, or eggplant parmesan, or lasagna. Nothing fancy, but always good with a garden salad (made with greens from our own composted garden).

So, on Saturdays, I usually walk down the hill for Ethiopian food.

I am quite fond of "*injera* and *wat*." Injera, made with a teff flour batter, is like a large spongy pancake. Wat is a spicy stew. My favorite is made with chicken. Beef and lamb are also options. During fasts, the choices are limited to stews made with lentils or chickpeas, without butter.

I've had a few lessons from Ethiopian women on how to prepare ingredients and cook the batter for injera. There's an art to pouring the batter on the flat, round griddle over an open fire. You start pouring around the outer edge and end in the center.

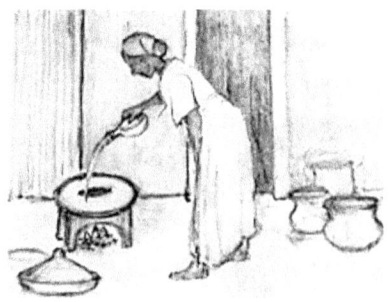

Cooking Injera.
Student artwork by Mosissa B.

The stews require chopping a lot of onions and squeezing out the liquid before cooking. The onions are then cooked in a clarified and spiced butter. Then the ground spices are added, followed by the meat or vegetables, all cooked slowly. Water can be added if necessary.

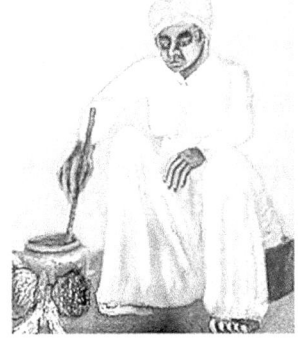

At Home, Grandmother stirs the Wat
Painting by student Mossisa B.

I have recipes with specific amounts and steps written down. The challenge back home may be finding the spices. I think Ethiopian food will be the thing I miss most after we leave here.

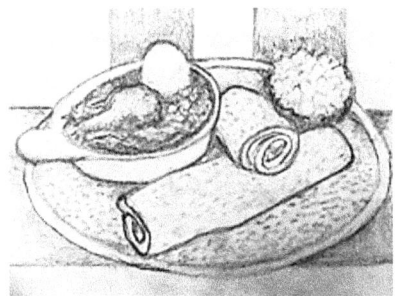

Doro Wat — Chicken leg and hardboiled egg
in a spicy onion sauce with injera and a bowl of cheese curd

May 15, 1964

Ishi nega. Amharic for "OK, tomorrow." It will get done tomorrow, or the next day, or the day after that. Putting things off until another day. It's a cultural thing.

But not always at Harar Teacher Training School.

Some decisions are made swiftly and discreetly.

Take last week, for example. One of my senior students did not show up for class two mornings in a row. He never missed class. He was especially talented in art as well as languages. He was conversant in seven. And incidentally, he was quite handsome and always well dressed. I considered him to be on track to be an outstanding teacher — skill, poise, presence, personality to spare until the following revelation:

"So where is he" I asked another student. "Is he sick?"

"He is gone, sir. He will not be coming back."

"Wait. What? Why?"

"He was trying to take a young girl's virginity. She was refusing him."

"How do you know this?"

"The warden saw it all happen. He stopped it and reported him to the director. They sent him home immediately."

"Oh, no. He was so talented. He seemed like such a nice guy."

"No, sir. You did not know him well. In the dorm, he boasted about his ability to deflower beautiful young girls. Each conquest was, I think the expression you use sir is, 'another notch on his belt.'"

"You're right. I guess I did not know him. If what you say is true, he certainly did not belong in the teaching profession. By the way, speaking of teaching, I still have not seen your lesson plan for the class you will be teaching at the model school next week."

"*Ishi nega*, sir, *ishi nega*."

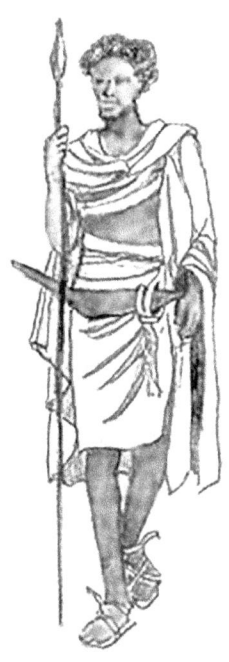

No Belt, No Notches.

June 13, 1964

Behaving Out of Character —
The Ogaden Basin is a region in eastern Ethiopia bordering Somalia. It is basically a Somali enclave in Ethiopia. Because there are frequent conflicts between the Ethiopian and Somalian armies over control of the Ogaden, the whole area is off limits to Peace Corps Volunteers unless accompanied by the U.S. Military Assistant Group.

Harar is about 100 miles from the Somalia border and about 60 miles from the town of Jigjiga, on the Ogaden boundary.

Jigjiga is just a two-hour bus ride from Harar. Very tempting.

So last weekend, Mike and I grabbed our backpacks and caught the Saturday morning bus to Jigjiga. We walked through the town and outdoor market. We spent the night at a decent hotel and returned to Harar on Sunday.

Why did we take the risk? Adrenalin rush? Because it was there?

The most interesting thing to me was the number of market stalls selling beautifully crafted knives. Not something one could find in our Harar markets, and not something I would feel comfortable carrying on the bus.

So, no souvenirs.

June 19, 1964

We had our open house at the school this weekend.

The art club had an exhibition of drawings, paintings, and crafts, including furniture, toys, and musical instruments. A real eye opener for the community.

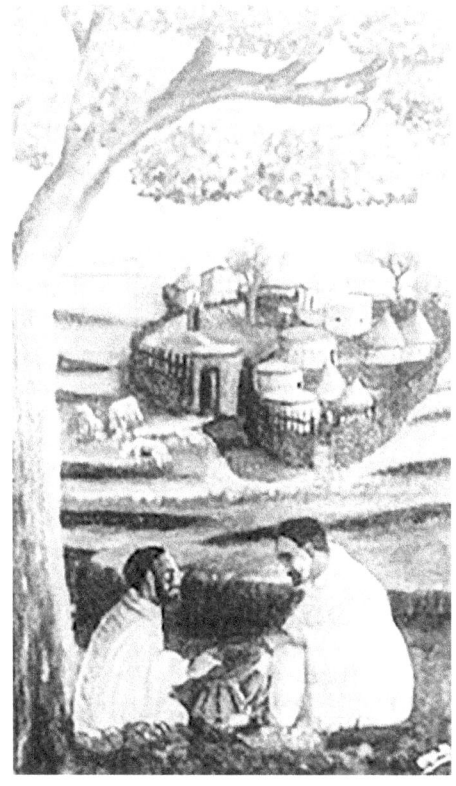

Playing the Game of Macala
Painting by student Teklehaimanot R.

We sold most of the artwork on display: horn-craft, baskets, woodcraft, leather, fiber-craft, drawings and paintings, watercolors and oils.

We had made our own watercolor with local pigment and egg yolk. We made our own oil paint with local pigment, drying oil and varnish.

The students received 80% of the selling price. The other 20% went to the school for art supplies.

When I first came here, I was discouraged. Very few students had a background in art, or even an awareness of their rich art heritage. As I look back on the past two years, I am pleased with the progress the students have made. On the days I walk to school, little children join me along the way.

They stop off at their school and wait for me to return.

I'd like to think that these children will remember that on these walks an American Peace Corps Volunteer taught them new words in English, told them stories, and drew pictures with them in the dirt.

Rimbaud's Harar

Bewitching Harar
Fabled home of tormented French poet
Arthur Rimbaud
Photographer, explorer, entrepreneur, coffee trader
Gun runner for Ethiopian King Menelik II
Too young and gifted to die at 37
Too reckless and riddled with pain to live.
Beguiling Harar
Rich with plush velvet, riotous colors, seductive scents
A tintinnabulation of sounds
An opiate for the pain of Rimbaud
Bewitched and beguiled by Harar.

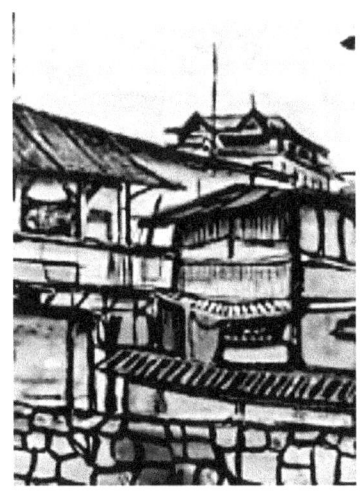

Rimbaud's House (top, background)

"Let it come, let it come
The day when hearts love as one."

ARTHUR RIMBAUD, FROM "A SEASON IN HELL" – 1873

June 29, 1964

Graduation was this past weekend. The night before, the faculty had dinner with the graduating class of 90 students. After dinner the students presented a program of folk dances and music from different provinces, followed by an original drama about problems they would face when teaching in remote villages. There were elements of tragedy laced with comedy.

It turns out they are going to face far more difficult situations than we as Peace Corps Volunteers ever would. The students are aware of the hardships they will face: no books, no classrooms, no chalkboards, no desks, no supplies, loneliness, being the only educated man or woman in the village, with no one to marry.

In one humorous skit, the men gave special thanks to Miss Damon for initiating Saturday cooking and sewing classes for men, since they are doomed to be bachelors and will have to take care of themselves.

In a beautiful, poetic way they said goodbye to TTS, calling it "The Mother School" they will be leaving behind, and to the Peace Corps Volunteers, who will, in a matter of days, be leaving it behind as well.

Traveler
by student Getachew T.

July 1, 1964

Some things end abruptly.

Our students all left the day after graduation.

Most were on the same night train to Addis Ababa.

From there, they will scatter by bus in every direction.

Some things end gradually.

The Harar PCVs, will be leaving one or two at a time, over a two-week period, depending on travel connections.

Some plan to fly east through Asia. One will visit South Africa, before flying home. One will have a layover in West Africa. A few are flying north through Europe. Most wanted to fly directly home. However, one of our group wants to stay behind, permanently.

Some things end reluctantly.

As for me, having visited the headwaters of both the Blue and White Nile rivers, well, Richard and I plan to follow the Great Nile River flowing north through Sudan and Egypt to its Mediterranean end.

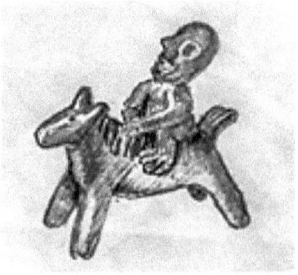

Student drawing by Saleh M. of a clay Falasha fetish

A Sense of Ending

At journey's end
The wake of the setting sun
Ignites the hills of memory
For one last time
With reflections
On life's noble pursuits
Simple deeds
Ordinary accomplishments
And humbling failures
Creating beauty
In the landscape
Of our minds.

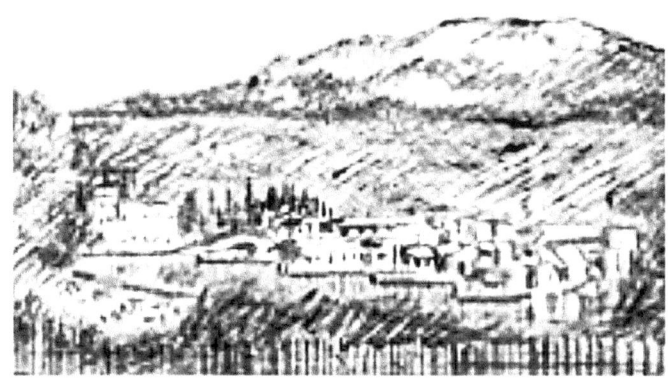

The Sun Sets on Harar

Days Pass

Slowly
Step by step
Layer upon layer
Choice after choice
Experience becomes life
Destiny is shaped and reshaped
As small acts, big risks, subtle changes
Broaden the arc of our life-journey's path.

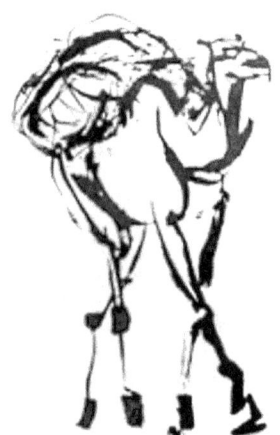

Subtle changes go more or less unnoticed
One living form taking from another.
Fragments merge, meld, evolve
Into uniquely hybrid forms
Generating strength
Renewed energy
As days pass
Quickly

HEADING HOME —
JULY 3 - AUGUST 3, 1964

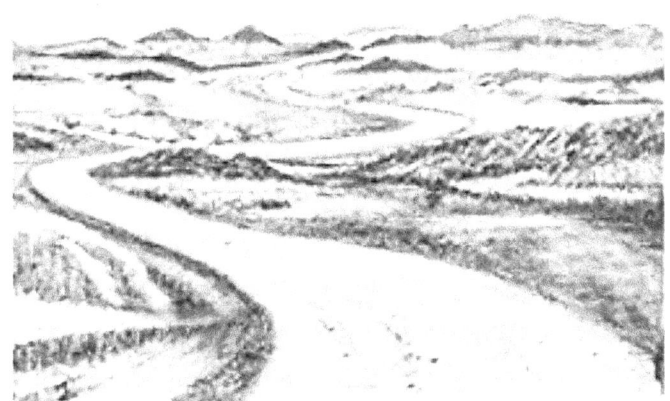

The Nubian Desert in Northern Sudan

Across the sands of time
Through lands once ruled by sultans, pharaohs and emperors
With oral traditions in rhythm and rhyme
Over the routes of explorers and conquerors
From the source of the Blue Nile
To the place of the Great Confluence
North down the Great Nile River
To the Mediterranean Sea.

Tales of Two Cities

Twin cities: Khartoum and Omdurman
Place of the Great Confluence
Where the chocolate-brown waters of the Blue Nile
Join the milky-blue waters of the White Nile
To form the Great Nile River
 A source of vital irrigation.

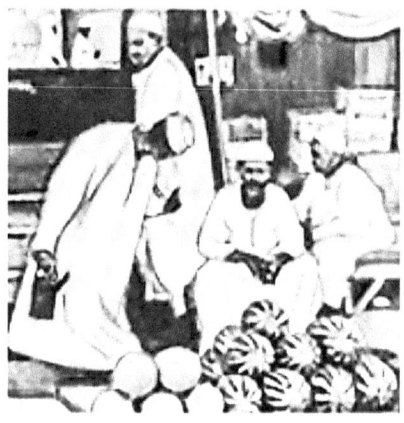

Twin cities: Nucleus of Sudan's population
Place of trade and commerce
Where melons are sold on every street corner
For nutrition and hydration.

Twin cities: Christian and Muslim
Place of conflict and strife
Where, in the 19th Century,
British and Ottoman Empire forces fell
To the swords of Mohammad Ahmad, the Mahdi
And where he later died in 1885

Khartoum —
A European built city.
Hot and dusty. No rain showers.
An early morning city, a night city.
Asleep during afternoon hours.

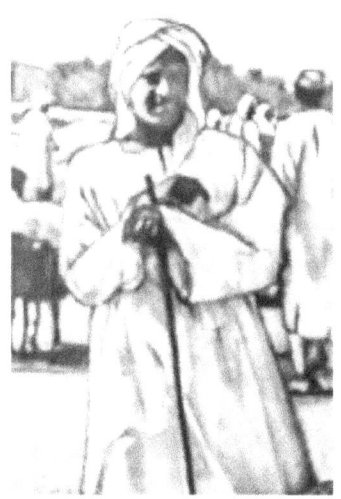

Counting Sheep in Omdurman

Omdurman —
An Arab built city.
Sand swept streets. Curtains drawn.
A low city, a mud brick city.
Awake before dawn.

An Expanse of No Cities

Nubian Desert —
Naked white sand
Bare black rock
As far as the eye can see.
No cities. No towns. No villages.
No places to eat or shelters to sleep.
Who dares to cross the desert alone
Except on a plane?

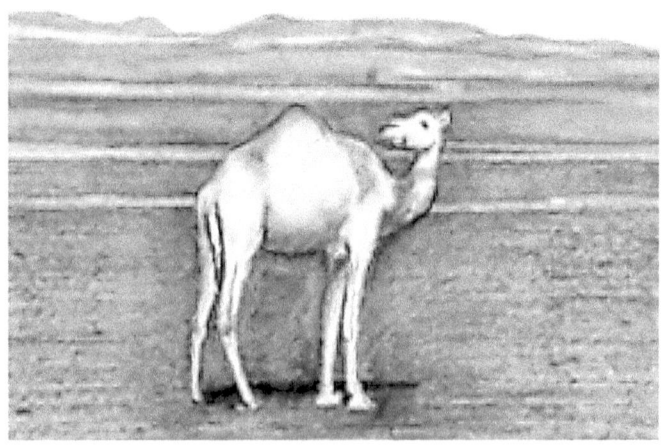

"Where did everybody go?"

Waiting in a Wadi

Wadi — (A dry river valley.)
A line of date palms in stoic order
On the horizon
Signals the Nile River once again.
Wadi Halfa is near Sudan's northern border with Egypt.
Things to do in Wadi Halfa:
Sleep.
Eat dates.
Wait for steamboats
To go North, down the Nile into Egypt
To go South, up the Nile into the Sudd.
Sudd — (A swampy lowland.)
It's only a matter of time,
A month perhaps,
Before the waters of the Nile,
Held back by the Aswan High Dam,
Will cover the town and the palm tree
Under which I sit
Eating dates,
Waiting for the last steamboat.

The Last Steamboat

Riding down the Nile
On the last steamboat
To depart from Wadi Haifa.
An overnight passage to Aswan
With comfortable upper cabins
And a crowded lower deck.

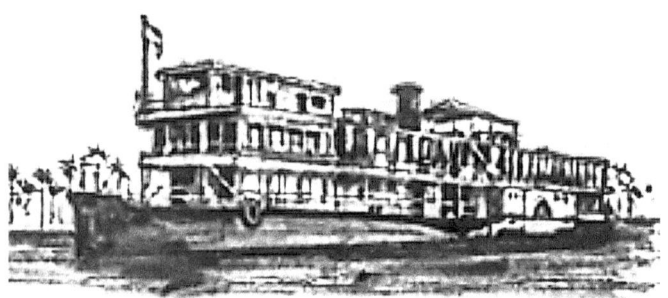

The Last Steamboat

Passing evacuated villages.
Sudanese and Egyptian governments are relocating
Entire villages of people to higher land
Far away from the banks
Soon to be submerged
By man-made Lake Nasser.

Abu Simbel & Aswan High Dam

In the pre-dawn hours
Four colossal statues of Ramses II
Emerge from the shadows
Towering with awe-inspiring grandeur
Over swirling river waters.
The statues form the facade
Of a great temple
Carved into a sandstone cliff
On the west bank of the Nile.
This too will be moved to higher ground.

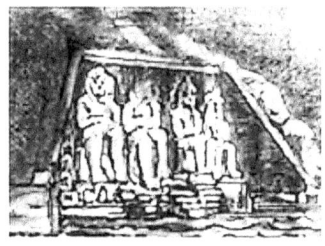

Ramses Quartet of Abu Simbel

Shella Aswan—
The Aswan High Dam,
In final stage of construction,
Comes into view.
The steamboat can go no further.
Job seekers clad in pima cotton *galabaya*
Break line to greet disembarking passengers
With hard bartering, gentle begging.
The hardship of desert life can be seen
In their leathered faces with deep-set eyes.

A Few Days in Cairo

In Cairo one can —
Enjoy the comforts of modern life
While admiring the magnificent inheritance
Of a glorious past.
Visit the Egyptian Museum
Surrounded by antiquity
See the cherished treasures of
King Tut's tomb.
Visit the Citadel, the Mosque of Mohammed Ali
The Blue Mosque and the Sultan Hassan Mosque.
Admire the designs of
Traditional craftsmen
Inlays of marble and alabaster
Wood, bone and ivory
Persian carpets, intricate geometrical patterns on
Walls, floors, ceilings, tessellated blocks.
Tip-toe shoeless in these great halls of prayer
Embarrassed by holes in your socks.
Visit the Pyramids at Giza and Memphis
Crawl inside the innermost chambers of these
Monumental tombs
Sense what it might be like to be entombed alive.
Ponder the battered face of the Great Sphinx.

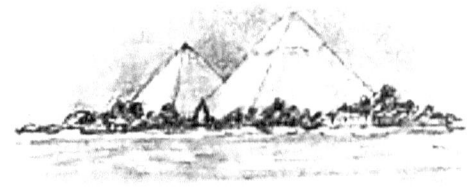

Iconic Pyramids

Alexandria
—
The Pearl of the Mediterranean

A bus ride completes the journey
To the delta of the Nile
To breath at last
The salt sea air
And swim
In azure
Water.
Two days
To explore Alexandria,
With jasmine in full bloom
Staying in what was formerly
King Farouk's Montazah Palace
With a pristine beach and lush garden
Overlooking the sparkling blue Mediterranean Sea.

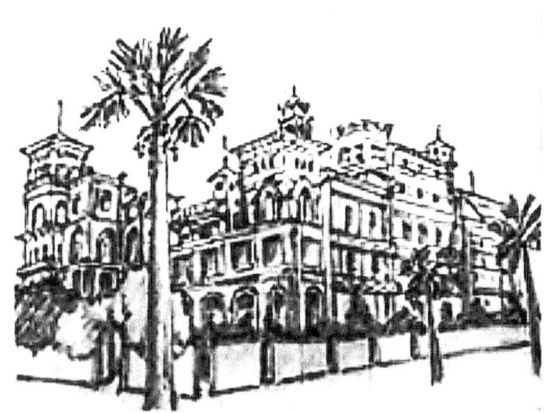

King Farouk's Montazah Palace

Amman

In Amman,
Once called Philadelphia
Now called "The White Pigeon,"
Jordanians have perfected the
Gentle art of pigeon keeping.
Flocks of brown,
Black, blue, gray
And white pigeons
Swoop and circle
In tight arcs
Returning home
At sunset.

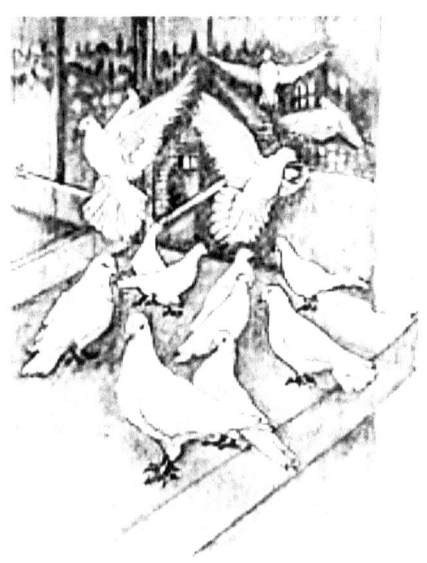

Jordanian Cote of White Pigeons

Jerusalem

A
Shrine
Sits among
Gnarled olive trees
Dating back to antiquity
Their roots firmly bound
To a rugged, rocky hillside.
If trees could talk, they would tell of the
Countless struggles of Muslims, Jews, Christians
English, Turks, Romans, Israelis, Palestinians
To possess these historic hallowed grounds

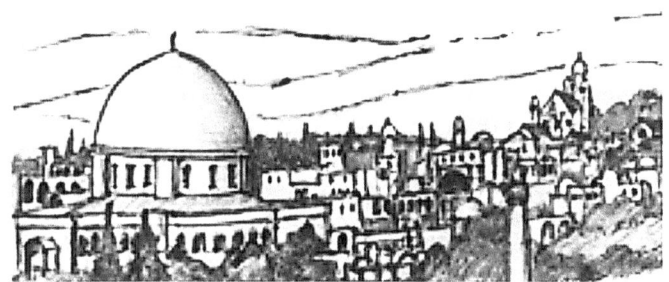

The Land of Canaan, The Promise Land
The Land of Milk and Honey
The Holy Land

Istanbul

Once Byzantium
Later Constantinople
Now a major Turkish city
Straddling the Bosporus Strait
Which separates Europe and Asia.
A vibrant blend of cultures
Where East meets West
In a crowded Bazaar
Or Hagia Sophia

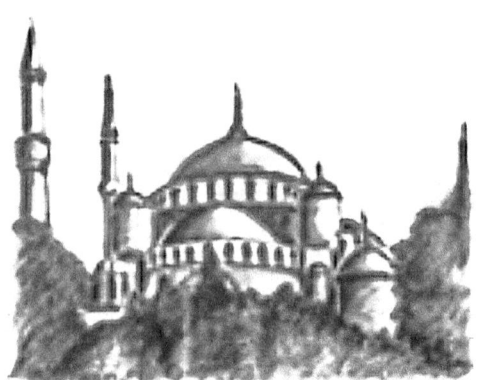

Hagia Sophia

Athens

The Parthenon glows
As first light caresses
Its fluted columns.
The aging wonder
Atop the Acropolis
Welcomes a new day.

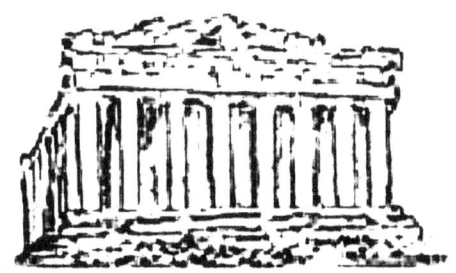

The Parthenon

An Afternoon at the Theatre

The Theatre of Epidaurus
A visual and auditory delight
A Hellenistic wonder
Adored for its aesthetics
Acclaimed for its acoustics
Still staging classic productions
Aeschylus's
The Suppliant Women
First performed 470 BC.
The first recorded use of the word
DEMOCRACY
Was in this Greek drama.

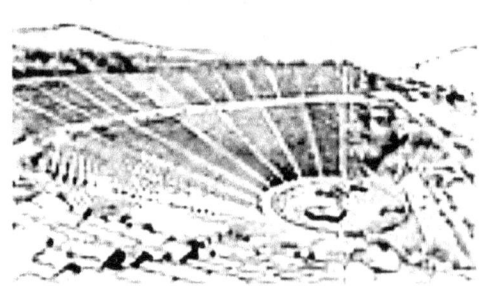

The Theatre of Epidaurus

One

being one
in a democracy
no one goes it alone
whether we win or lose
we are greatest together
respectful of one another
we are stronger together
mindful of compromise
we are bolder together
revengeful to none
when we are
one

Mediterranean Blues

Seas of clear water
Isolating Greek islands
Pure azure blue

Hillsides of olives
Fields of oregano, sage
And lavender blue

Black/white sand beaches
Sunlight on white-washed houses
Trimmed in indigo blue

Grecian island sky
Clear, cloudless expanse of bright
Cerulean blue

Scattered rays of sun
Dissolved in salty water
Is this why
The Mediterranean Sea
Is so very
blue?

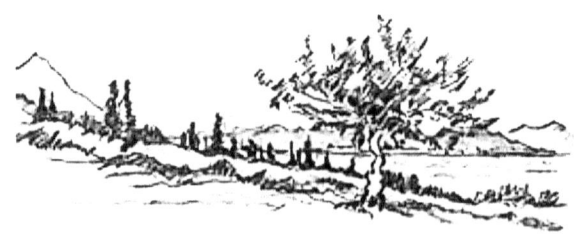

Olive Tree

Rome

Walk in time's footsteps
Admiring Roman wonders
Art, architecture
See now
Imagine then
How things might have looked
How things might have been
When they were new

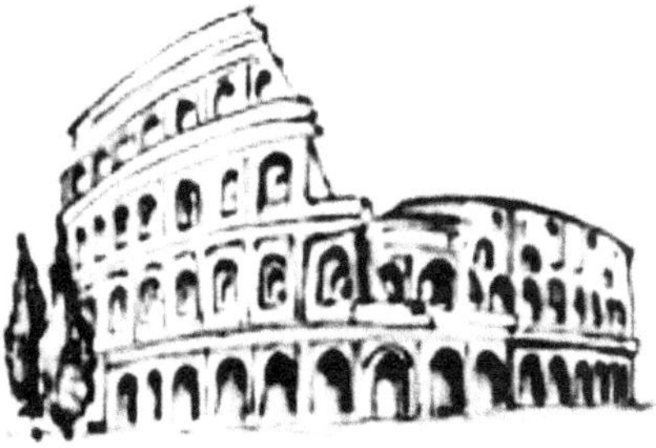

The Flavian Amphitheater

A pantheon, a colosseum
A forum, a fountain
A ceiling in a chapel
Imagine painting flat on your back
As in bed
With wet plaster overhead
Dine alfresco every night
In a private garden or crowded piazza
After four days of antiquity
Spend one last night at the opera
Aida
Under the stars
At the Baths of Caracalla

Empires implode
Monuments crumble
People destroy, people rebuild
People conquer, people fall
We are not perfect
We are human
But the great ideas
Ideals and spirit of humanity live on
Thriving like the cats of Rome.

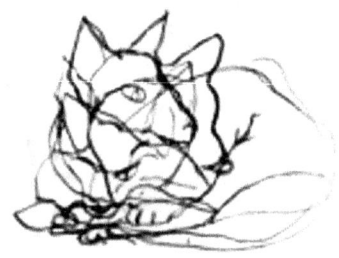

Nine lives or multiple personalities?

No more delays.
No more diversions.
This is it.
I sit alone.
Who goes home?
Who stays behind?
Ethiopia still
Weighs heavily on my mind.
What memories will be silenced?
What ideas will be carried home?
A lot to decide on my flight
From Rome.

RE-ENTRY – A YEAR OF ADJUSTMENTS

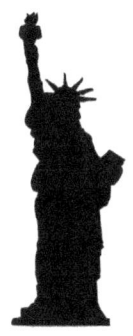

Symbol of Place

How do you symbolize a place
Where many come with style and grace,
Though victimized, tired and often poor,
Wanting asylum, safety and nothing more
Than liberty.
What crown can show equality
When some are denied that destiny?
What broken chain can show that all are free
When some, it seems, will never be?
What torch can show the way to peace
When hate speech seems to never cease?
What document can show that laws are just
When lie after lie instills mistrust?
What symbols speak for you and me
"I'm proud to be . . ."?

Looking for Shadows

I look for shadows in the night
Shadows long and deep
To help me fall asleep
I look for shadows in moonlight
Shadows that dance
Evoking memory of romance
I look for shadows out of sight
With potential for eerie fright
I look for shadows of my life
Shadows of self, of me
Shadows where I could never be
I look for shadows in sunlight
Shadows behind me that remind me
Shadows beside me that guide me
Shadows ahead of me instead of me
I look for shadows that fade
I look for shadows no longer there
I look for shadows that never were

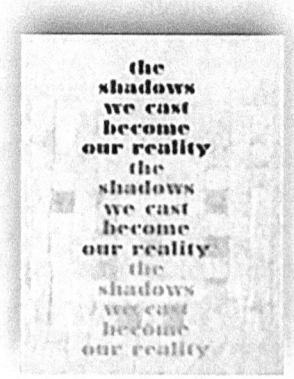

Readjusting

Volunteering in a foreign land,
Putting one's career on hold
In service to one's country,
Is a stressful challenge
But no less so than
Re-entry,
Coming home
To former colleagues,
Unaware of the sacrifices made,
Who seem unappreciative and taciturn
Reluctant to make sacrifices in return.
Living and working
In a developing country.
While personally rewarding and fulfilling,
Can be risky, stressful and chilling.
But as overwhelming as life overseas can be,
Returning home to a complex society
Is even more overwhelming
Than some may foresee.
Whether risking one's life in war,
Or volunteering one's service in peace,
Coming home after extended tours abroad
Can be stressful to say the least.
First there is shock at comfort and selfishness
Followed by awareness of polarizing divisiveness.
Then comes adjustments and decisiveness
But never complete contentment.
There will always be,
Or so it seems,
Ambivalence . . . shadows . . . dreams

You Never Asked

Are you okay?
How can there be conversation
When everyone is talking
So, when I speak
The sky listens
My words
Drifting like clouds
So, when I ask
The sky listens
My questions
Wafting like wind
And when I am silent
The sky hears
My thoughts
My words billowing in the clouds
My stories scattered among the stars
Because I never told
Because no one ever asked
Are you okay?

The Sky Listens

No One Goes It Alone

Life is a challenge
To be shared with others
In all we do.
For we have always known
No one goes it alone.
Relationships
With all people
Not just an elite few
Are equal.
The well being
Of all people
Not just an elite few
Is of primary importance.
For we have always known
It takes a village.
No one goes it alone.

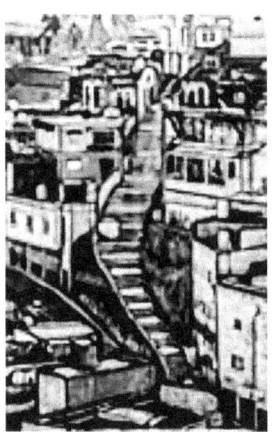

The City of Stairs

Take A Closer Look

Take a closer look at your visual world.
Know it sensitively
Feel its many textures
Examine its structures
Uncover its varied forms
Experience its energies, its mysteries
Its warmth, its complexities.
Take a closer look at details.

Take a closer look at your visual world.
Know it intimately
Sense its subtle changes
Study relationships in color
Search for patterns in things familiar
Compare rhythms and cycles of its life forms
Enjoy its diversity, its grandeur, its extremes, its intricacies.

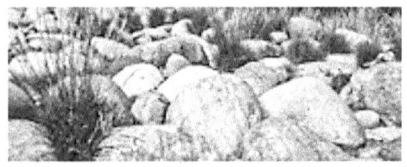

Take a closer look at the particulars.
Look closely at your visual world.
Know it specifically
Follow its paths of line and movement
Enter its places
Explore spaces for shelter, for play, for work, for meditation
Wonder about the regiment of form and order
Ponder balance, informality, voids, familiarities.

Take a closer look at specifics.
Look closely at your visual world.
Know it passionately
Find harmony in human activity
Investigate the rituals and celebrations of life
Seek meaning in human experience
Pursue the depth and forms of feeling
Consider loneliness, ecstasy, strength, vulnerabilities.

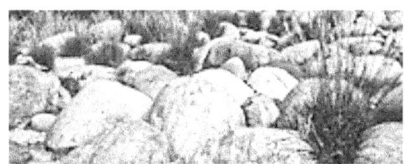

Take a closer look at relationships.
Look closely at your visual world.
Know it symbolically
Learn its language
Manipulate its materials
Use its tools of expression
Give form to your feelings
Tolerate the planned, the accidental
The comforting, the uncertainties.

Take a closer look.
Then take a second look.
Discover your visual world.
Discover its possibilities.
Discover yourself.

FIRM FOUNDATIONS

In layers
Step by step
Phase by phase
We build our lives
On the foundation of
Faith, family and fitness.
But at any time
Our firm footing can be thrown off balance
By unexpected events that crack the mortar of certainty
And pave the way for transformation and reconnection.

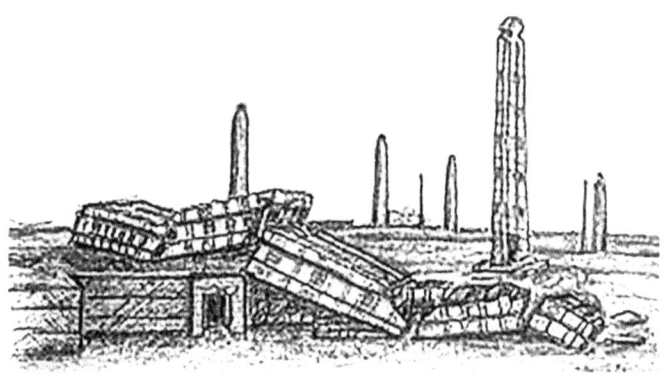

The Broken Stele of Axum

A Most Appropriate Post-Peace Corps Wedding

Adrienne Damon and I were both Peace Corps Volunteers teaching in the same school in Harar, Ethiopia, 1962-64. We were married on Cape Cod, MA, June 19, 1965. One week later we were in training in New York City at Teachers College, Columbia University for a Teacher Education in East Africa Project funded by the Agency for International Development.

Eight weeks later we were living in Kampala, Uganda. Fifty-four years later we are still together.

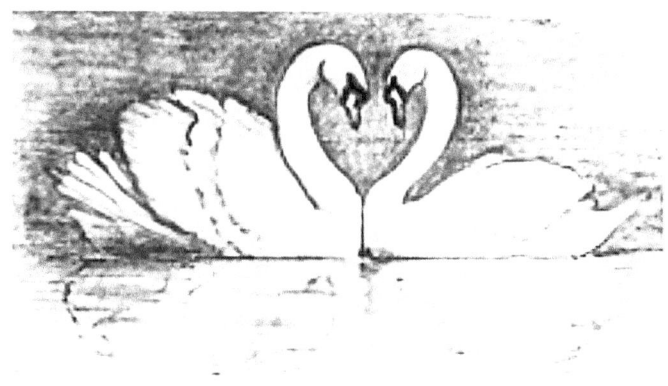

"Truth may walk through the world unarmed."

BEDOUIN PROVERB

THE POST-PEACE CORPS YEARS
—
GLOBAL PURSUITS

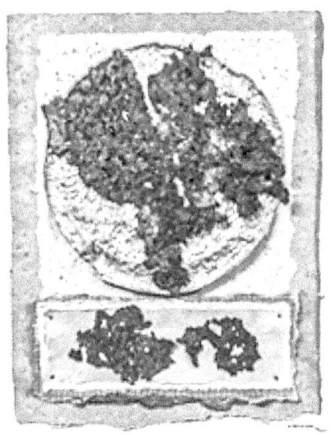

Continental Drift
Handmade paper & rusted metal

One world, many continents
Drifting apart
One nation, divisible by isms
Drifting apart
One people, marred by intolerance
Drifting apart
One earth, scorched, adrift

In Pursuit of Common Good

Naive journeyers know not
Where their footsteps will lead.
Embraced by karma
They shape their destiny through small actions
Mere sketches of life
Along a road of discovery
That becomes a global pursuit.
Global pursuits
Are propelled forward by
Risk, failure, rejection
Stamina, success, reflection
Humor, compromise, negotiation
In pursuit of common good.

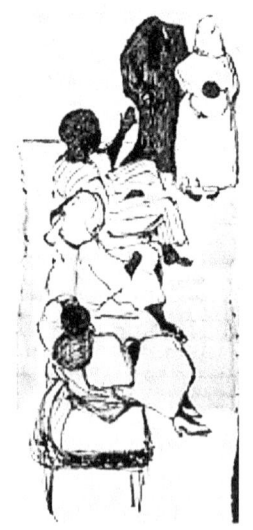

Midnight in the Bamako Airport

NOTES FROM UGANDA: 1965-1967

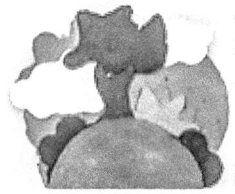

Two Years of Living on the Equator

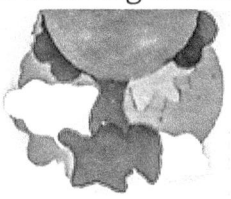

Precise + Pleasant
The predictability of weather patterns
The regularity of temperatures
The persistence of pythons
The prevalence of geckos
The constancy of days
The illusion of calm

Perfunctory + Poignant
The puzzlement of tribal unrest
The instability of political conflict
The upheaval of earthquakes
The precaution of curfews
The peril of rebellion
Inevitable coup

Eyes, Hands & Minds on Art

How good are you at seeing?
Sometimes we take looking for granted
See lazily, too tired to focus.
Everyday objects lose meaning beyond use.

How good are you at touching?
Sometimes we take touch for granted
Manipulate clumsily, unable to control our hands.
The things we make lose meaning beyond completion.

How good are you at analyzing?
Sometimes we take reasoning for granted
Think narrowly, unwilling to open our minds.
Events in the world lose significance beyond commentary.

How much do you appreciate art?
Sometimes we take art for granted
Dismiss the importance of its existence.
Works of art lose meaning and significance in our lives.

Perhaps we only start to value art
When we connect eyes, hands, and minds
Consider more than short-cut methods
Consider more than outer appearances.

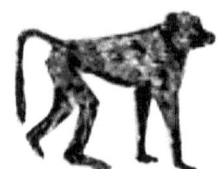

Functions of Art

Every day and in all seasons
People make art for different reasons
But everywhere in our vast global maze
Art functions for all in similar ways

There's a personal function of art
Expressing feelings of the heart
Communicating thoughts profound and fanciful
Recording what is seen as beautiful

Art has a role that's spiritual
Facilitating a belief system's ritual
Creating atmospheres for meditation
Providing inner-peace and contemplation

Art also has a cultural side
Promoting social values and civic pride
Commemorating historic events and glories
Honoring heroes and telling their stories

By far the most practical role of art
Planning a process from the start
Working skillfully is how one succeeds
Designing products for basic needs

There's a human urge for decoration
Enhancing moods for festive celebration
Embellishing objects with trim and ornament
Beautification, prettification, and adornment

Kiganda Gothic

When seekers meander
Through lush green groves of banana trees
In the cool Uganda highlands
They emerge much later
Through a dense canopy
Of Gothic style archways
As enlightened ones
In a state of tranquility.

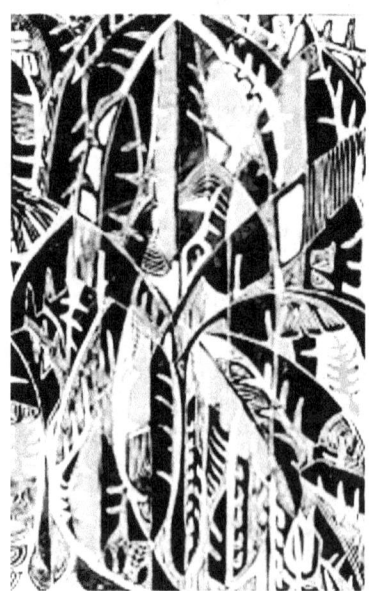

Kiganda Gothic.Woodcut

Day After Day

Walking
Day after day
Into the fields
Women
Working morn to night
Bundling the hay
Reaping the yields
Children
Digging the soil
Without play
Just days of endless toil
Mothers and daughters
Working side by side
Without pay, without a say
Walking with pride
Into the light.

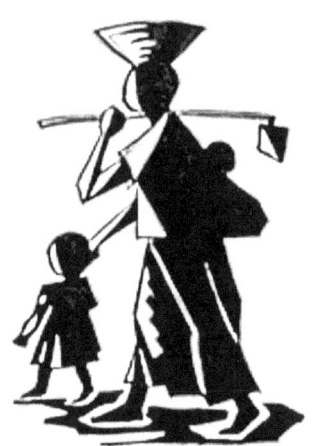

Into the Fields

Speaking Luganda

I like the rhythm of Luganda
Spoken with pneumatic tongue clicks
It'll take one quarter time
To set the tempo and rhyme
So, the beat can be tapped out with drumsticks.

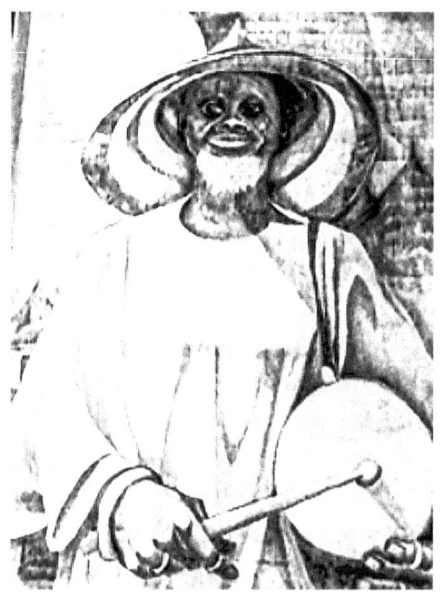

Beat the Drum Slowly

Mwango's Mangos

Mwango grows mangos
Mongooses eat mangos
Mangos grow wherever a mongoose goes
Where the mongoose goes
Mwango follows
Mwango sells mangos

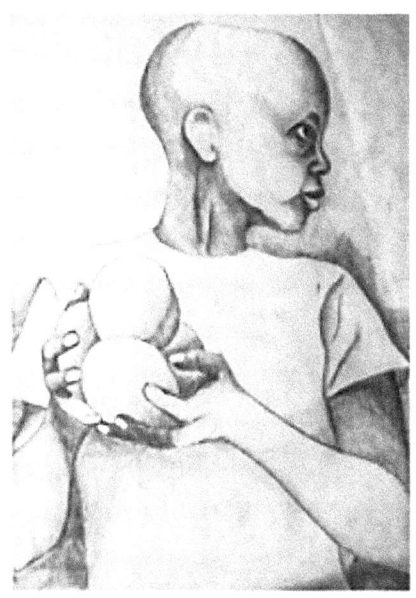

Mwango with Mangos at Kyambogo

Growing an Avocado in Kyambogo

Put the pit in a pot and pack with peat
Wet well with water, watch and wait
You don't want the roots to rot
The pit will split and sprout a sprig
A stem will soon shoot up
Before leaves pop out with bravado
That's how you grow an avocado
In Kyambogo

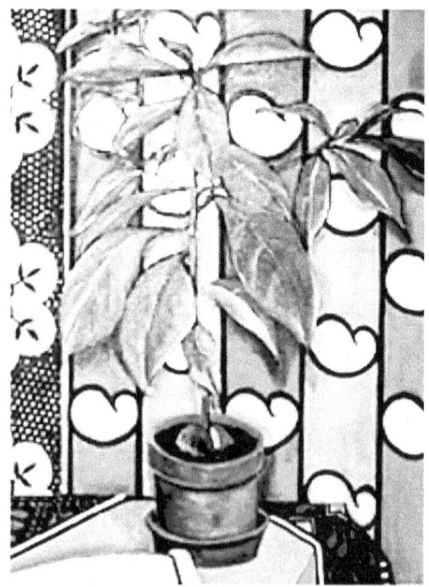

Avocado with Baganda Backdrop

It's Called Ugandan Courage

Relaxed and at ease
Resting under banana trees
Relishing the tropical breeze
Hoping to catch a few more zees
So please
Do no sneeze or wheeze
As you drink a shot of *enguli*
With a squeeze
Of *ugli*.
Enguli is made from fermented bananas,
And is marketed commercially as Waragi
(translation: "war gin").
It's called Ugandan courage.

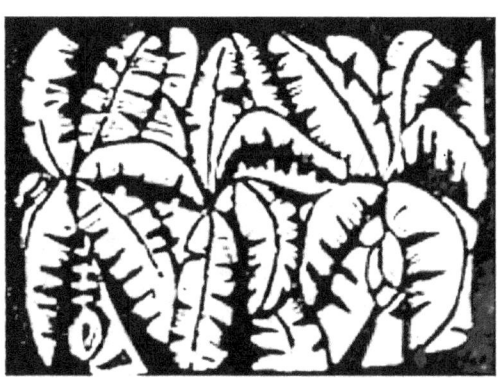

Baganda Banana. Lino Print

Revolution Road

They
Walked
Along the road
The man and a boy
And all they could see
Through the smoky haze
For miles and miles and miles
Were the ashes and charred
Remains of once lush
Sugar cane fields
Scorched earth
The final act
Of unjust
War.

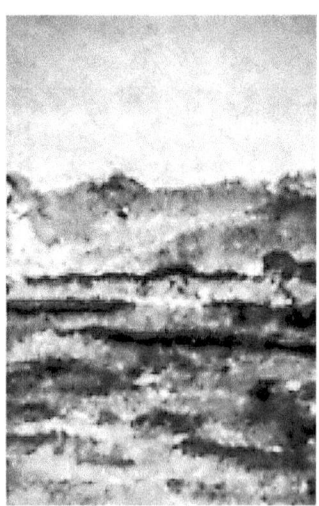

Burned paper landscape

Horrified and Hopeless

The man and a boy
Are searching for peace
Beyond the hostile expanse
Of burning remains of conflict
"Are we there yet?" asks the anxious child.
"Not quite" says the man "but it's on the horizon."
"How far away might that be?" asks the curious child.
The man answers with a hesitant air of finality,
"I don't know. No one has ever reached it"

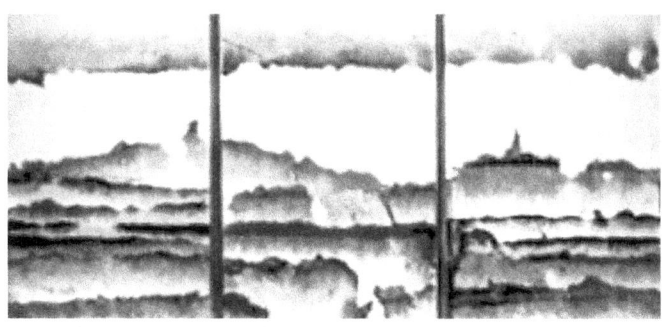

A coup by the army, led by Idi Amin, put Milton Obote in power and exiled Sir Edward Mutesa to London. The coup ended and the months-long curfew was lifted November 1, 1966, the day our first daughter was born at Mulago Hospital in Kampala, Uganda. Six months later we terminated our contract and returned to the United States. Six years later, Idi Amin was in charge, and the basement of Mulago Hospital became a torture chamber.

We Await Our Fate

Banishment or punishment
We await our fate
We are those without a voice
We are those denied a choice
Disenfranchised
Exiled or executed
We await our fate
We are those who may have strayed
We are those who feel betrayed
Dispossessed
Shunned or shackled
We await our fate
We are the uneducated
Those who feel segregated
Marginalized
Interned or incriminated
We await our fate
We are those with checkered pasts
We are those with uncharted paths
Neglected

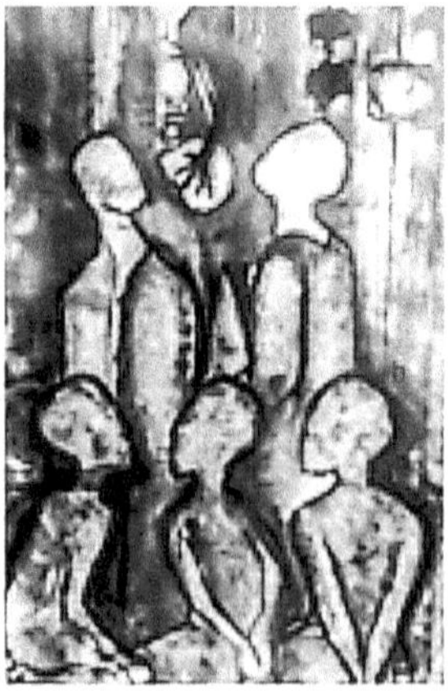

Anonymous People

Faces in shadow
Figures in light
Casually observed
Hidden from sight
Places forgotten
Detail slight
Anonymous people
Fade into the night.

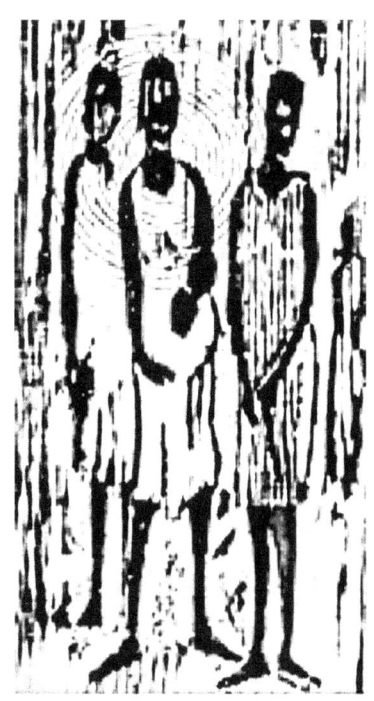

February 1967

East Africa Safari

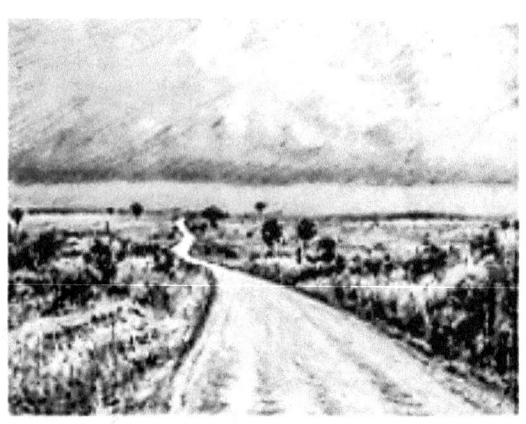

We crisscross the equator
And the vast Rift Valley
In our little Renault RoHo
With our eight-week old daughter Sara
Sleeping comfortably in a wooden crate
Strapped securely in the backseat
Beside Grandma Mary.
We backtrack the routes of early explorers
From Uganda into Kenya and Tanzania.
We drive around Mt. Kilimanjaro
Into Ngorongoro Crater.
Across the Serengeti
We wait long stretches of time
While herds of elephant and eland
Zebra and wildebeest cross the road.

YEARS LATER

NOTES FROM WEST AFRICA

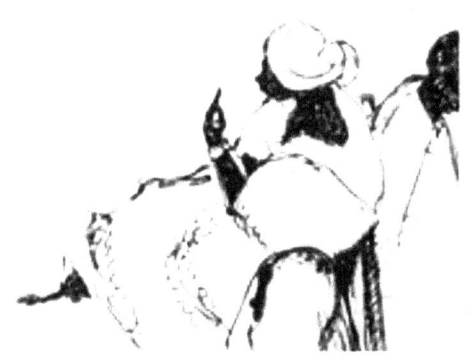

Waiting for a Flight in Bamako
Ball point pen

Every journey finds people
Waiting, watching, wondering
When better days will come.
Every journey is populated
With memorable faces
Striking features
Sensual forms.

A Night in Bamako

In a jumbled pile of red and green rubber flip-flops
Yellow jelly slip-ons and brown leather sandals
One lone blue shoe
Stands apart from the rest
Who does it belong to?
I'm in the airport lobby at midnight
Waiting for the next flight out
Noisy, sweltering hot
Crowded with people
Some in colorful robes, others not
Clusters of women with burkas on
Head and face covered
In shades of indigo, purple and ebon
A few sit on benches with backs
Others lounge on woven grass mats
Sharing bandana wrapped popcorn snacks
Everyone (but me) seems comfortable, cool and clean

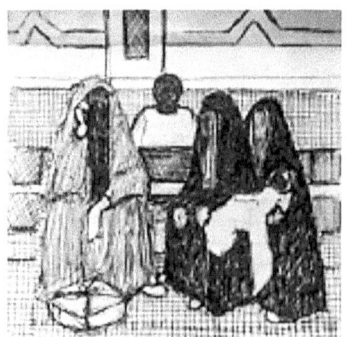

Waiting in Bamako
Ball point pen

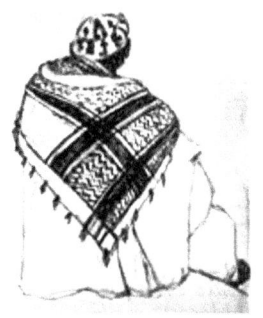

Waiting Patiently in Bamako

The slow motion of ceiling fans overhead
Brings swarms of termites with translucent wings
Flapping erratically as though just learning to fly
The number increasing as the night goes by
When they fall to the floor
Attendants scoop them up by the handful
Dropping them into buckets of water
Later to be roasted for a tasteful
Nutritious snack.

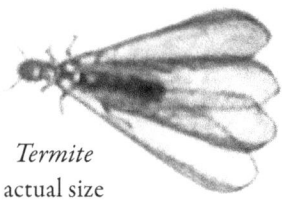

Termite
actual size

Though memories fade
Sketches remain unfinished on paper
As fragile, yellowing fragments
Of observation.

A Day in Dakar

Dakar
The most crowded airport by far
No lines
Just pushing, shoving, hoards
With parcels bound with sisal twines
Heading for a
Motorcar
Out on the street
Small boys grab onto your feet
Making it impossible to walk
All you can do is try to talk
Down the price they demand
For the jewelry they shove in your hand.

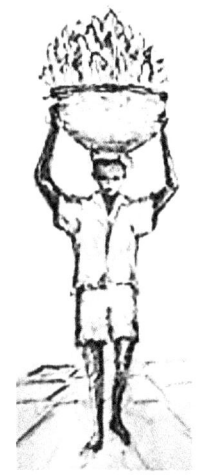

Street Vendor in Dakar

Mid-day in Niamey

Niger days
Interrupted by
Harmatan haze.
The big bright blue sky
Suddenly turns light blood-orange
Becoming dark rust.
Haboob

Cotton-candy cloud
Churning three hundred feet high
Carries desert sand.
Haboob

The powerful winds
Rattle cabin walls and floors
Hissing under doors.
Haboob

Wet towels jammed tight
Against the wide threshold cracks
Don't keep out the sand.
Haboob

Keep eyes closed, mouth shut
Get under bedcovers quick
Wait 'til the wind dies.
Haboob

Ten minutes or hours
Everything coated with grit
Even the soap bar . . .
And toilet.
Haboob

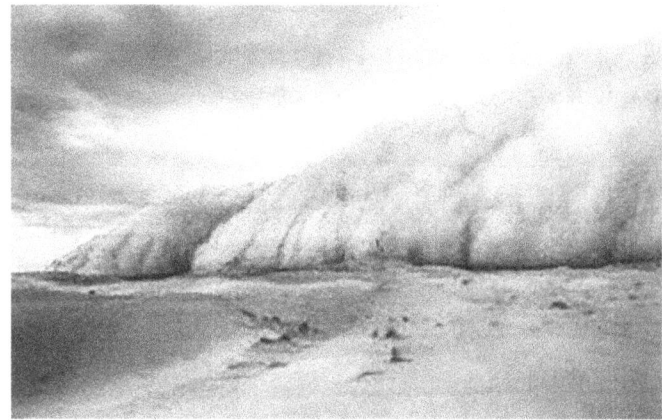

Haboob

Haboob – Saharan sandstorm
Harmattan – West African "winter" season

When There is More to a Door
There is More to Adore

A door does more than keep out the wind
It might speak of acceptance or rejection
Suggest a beginning or an ending
Hide a secret or reveal a truth.
There is always more to a door.
A door does more than keep out the sand
It might indicate caring or lack of concern
Suggest respect or disregard
Hide a mistake or reveal perfection.
There is always more to a door.
A door does more than protect us from harm
It might symbolize acceptance or exclusion
Suggest awareness or intolerance
Hide a bias or reveal hope.
There is always more to a door.
A door is more than an entrance or exit
It might be an opening to a world of wonder and awe
An adit to refine our sense and sensibilities
A portal to peace and understanding.
There is so much to adore.

Doors to Understanding

Look behind, see a world of despair.
Look straight ahead, see a doorway.
Look beyond, see possibilities to compare —
Possibly a portal to worship
Shrouded figures, muted prayer.
Possibly an entrance to a gravesite
Angelic trappings, silent stare.
Possibly a passage to a temple
Noble statues, altars bare.
Possibly a gateway to a city
Ancient walkways, market square.
Possibly a drawbridge to a castle
Regal symbols carved with care.
Once through the doorway:
Be fully aware.

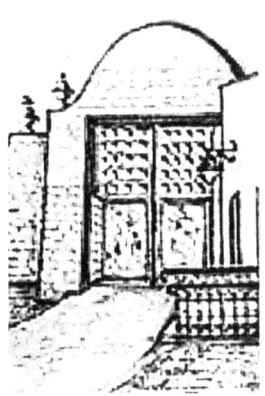

Seeking Solutions

When designers seek solutions
They are most assuredly inclined:
To investigate real problems
With specific purposes in mind;
To look for new approaches
With limits and constraints defined;
To consider possible adjustments
Leaving no plausible idea behind;
To identify measurements of progress
Allowing time to rest and rewind.
Design is a way of thinking about
Purpose, process, pitfalls, progress and product.

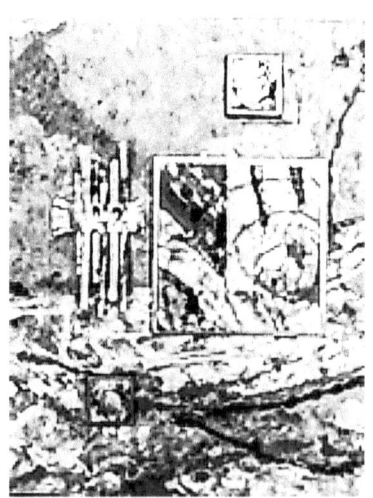

We Were Here First
Handmade paper

MANY YEARS LATER . . .

NOTES FROM THE MIDDLE EAST

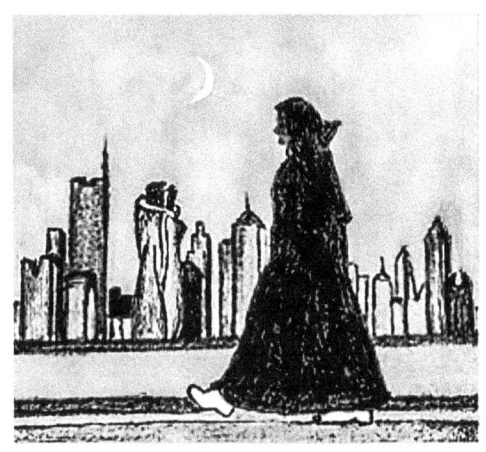

*Doing the Dusk Drill in Doha along the
Qatar Quay*

Don't be held hostage by the past.
 Yesterday's solutions are neither today's
 Nor tomorrow's.

A Few Days in Qatar
(to speak about what the arts do best)

. . .. And so, in closing, to all educators who have
An oral tradition of fine poetry, I offer a poem of my
own.
Apologetically, quite elementary:

Over time
Without symbols to remind,
Without stories to unwind,
Without beauty to find,
Our collective history,
Our varied cultures,
Our sense of self
All become a mystery,
Our past a false revision
Our future a shifted destiny
Of blind, cultural division,
Senseless oppression,
Slight omission.

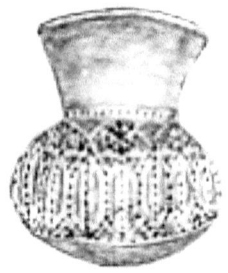

Pierced metal mosque lamp

Without the arts, what will remain to shape our humanity?

Doha
Pearl of the Persian Gulf

A night at the opera
At Katara Amphitheater
Followed by a night
At Al-Waiba Palace
Guest of Her Highness
The Amir's Consort
Minah Bint Nasser Al-Hissned
Feasting on:
Soup of artichokes with truffles
Lobster fricassee with diced vegetables
Fish Madrouba
Roasted pigeon flavored with orange chutney
And red pepper potatoes
Harris
Stick of three chocolate date ice cream
And hibiscus coulis

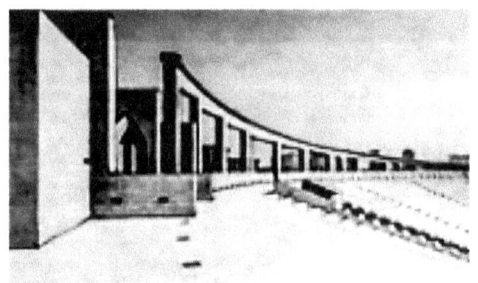

Katara Amphitheater. Doha

Keep Walking

Walk into the desert, inhale the heat
Walk over the dunes, endure the push of pain
Walk across the sand, feel the pull of emptiness
Walk amid rocky outcrops, welcome the shade
Walk toward the sunset, steady the stride
Feel the pull of vast, open space.
Keep walking.

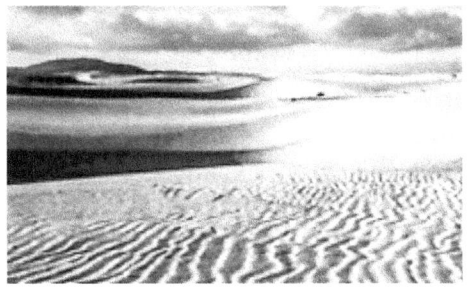

Qatar Desert

(Exhale, slowly)
We see the present
(Inhale, deeply)
Only as it is leaving us.
(Exhale)
Too soon for some
(Inhale)
Too late for others
(Exhale)
To move with grace.

Midnight Swim

Persian Gulf or Arabian Sea?
Just a very salty, buoyant body of water to me
Loaded with phosphorescence.
Swimming at midnight
Is like swimming among fireflies
Flickering in the water
As each stroke of the arm
Disturbs the brine.
Qatar pearls,
Tears of the mermaids,
Or exhausted state of mind?
Floating. Eyes wide open.
A slight crescent moon visible tonight.
Only pain to fight.
Drifting.
Warm salty water rises over my body.
Eyes now closed.
Exhaling.
No breathing.
Slowly sinking
Below the surface
For an eternity of mere seconds.
Gently willing the pain to sink deeper
Further away from my body.
Slowly rising into the warm night air
Gasping. Eyes opening.
Bright stars to greet me.
Qatar pearls,
Tears of angels,
Or tranquility?

Falconry

Hunting wild game
With trained birds of prey
Once a means of survival
Now the sport of sheikhs
An opulent, surreal spectacle.
Peregrine falcons
Naturally feathered
Unnaturally
Hooded and tethered
Then released to perform
Predatory aggression
Gracefully
In Qatar

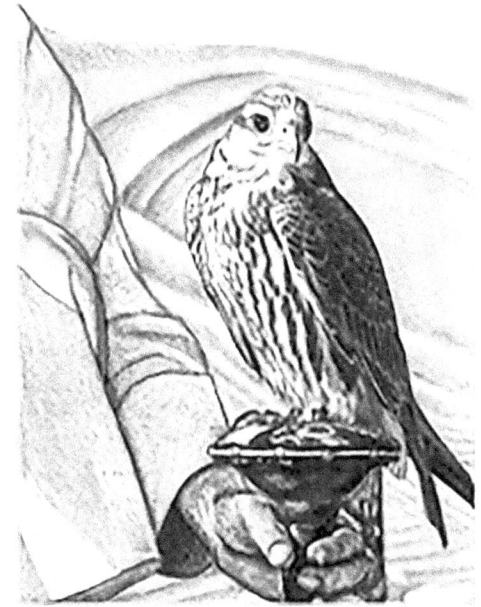

A Bird in Hand . . .

In-flight Lesson

Across the aisle
The old man watches me
Fasten my seat belt
Matching my every move
Signaling for approval
With raised eyebrows
Obviously, a first-time flyer
In business class.
When snacks come
I show him how to
Remove the plastic wrap from the tray.
He watches carefully
And does exactly what I do.
I take a bite from a finger sandwich.
So does he.
I squeeze a lemon wedge
Over the sliced salmon salad.
So does he.
I drop the rind into my soda.
So does he.
I smile.
So does he.

What Age Are We Living In?

Like the depth of glacier ice
The evolution of humanity
Goes unnoticed from day to day.
Like the movement of planets
The subtle shifts in morality
Are unfelt along the way.
Humankind moved out of the ice age
Through periods defined by rocks,
Metals, agriculture, writing, intellect,
Monarchs, industry, atoms, space,
Information and interaction.
But no one really knew
A major change was underway.
As we exploit, reshape and bend
The world around us to suit
A personal or evangelistic end
We rarely consider the long-term impact
Our self-interests and pursuits
May have on the expanding
Global village we now live in
And the connectedness
We have with all others.
And so, we are off balance
At odds with ourselves
Clueless as to the next
Yet unnamed age
We are creating.
Perhaps the age
Of incivility?

"Know the world in yourself.
Never look for yourself in the world."

EGYPTIAN PROVERB

AND ALL THE YEARS
IN BETWEEN . . . AND AFTER

BRINGING THE PEACE CORPS EXPERIENCE
BACK HOME

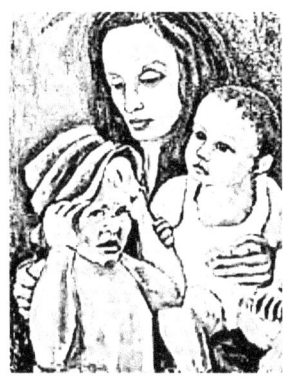

Family with More to Come

"... to learn peace,
    To live peace,
        And to labor for peace,
            From the beginning
                Of their service
                    To the end of their lives."
                        A Peace Corps mission statement

Establishing New Roots

For former Peace Corps Volunteers
The world eventually becomes
A space without borders
A connected place
A global village
A hometown
Open space
But sometimes
Even the most adventurous
Wanderers need to take a break
From purposeful global pursuits
To settle down and establish new roots
Knowing full well they may be "*auslanders*"
As we were first called when we settled in Kutztown
A Pennsylvania German town
Now our hometown
For very close to
Half a century

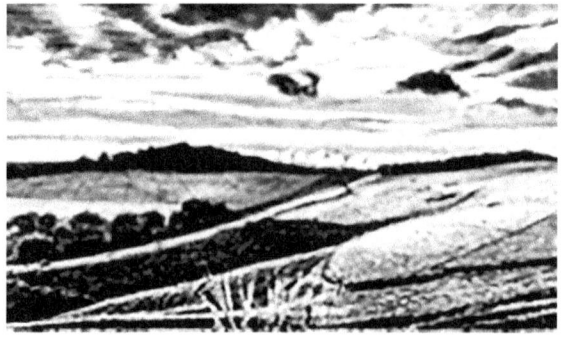

A Place to Set Down Roots

An Enduring Memory

A half century has passed yet the memories last
As we continue to share much from our Peace Corps past.
Our careers in education have been culturally enriched
By our days together as teachers in Ethiopia —
Returned Peace Corps Volunteers
Forever bewitched.

A half century has gone by, yet we wonder why
Memories of four decades as professional educators do not die.
Our careers in teaching moving along alternating tracks
At times involved with special populations
Special talents, special needs, special kids
On the verge of falling through the cracks

A half century of teaching is a startling admission
Whether working in public schools or higher education
Teaching kids in need of one-on-one remediation
Or preparing students for teacher certification
The commitment is the same — dedication

A half century seems so long ago, but a short time to show
How our belief in an exploration of humanistic goals
In public education seemed to take root and grow:
Learners involved in examining universal human experience,
Weighing diverse cultural influence,
Questioning personal preference
Testing informed judgments
Setting standards of
Excellence.

Artists and Teachers — Agents of Change

Artists learned to be agents of change long ago.
They knew one cannot become a butterfly by remaining
a caterpillar.
They creatively played with perception, illusion, and
distortion.
They imaginatively fooled around with reality, fantasy,
and myth.
They methodically explored relationships between science
and magic,
Between mind and spirit, between eye and hand in pursuit
of change.

Teachers, like artists, are also in pursuit of change.
Their students cannot become a butterfly by remaining a
caterpillar.
They know that opportunity, not ability, may stand in the
way.
OK, so it's a fact: People have a right to remain ignorant.
Yes, it's true: People are inclined to resist change,
Comfortable to stay with what they think they already
know is truth.
Thinking we already know enough for something to be
the truth
Prevents us from seeking other possibilities.
Believing we already know the truth limits new discoveries.

Teachers, by the nature of their job, are agents of change.
They transform the lives of their students,
Control chaos, alter reality, modify ideas,
Adapt techniques, and refine teaching styles
To develop an interest in learning —
An interest that will enable students
To ask questions
To learn how to learn
To continue to pursue facts
To learn new truths every day.
To become butterflies
To be a child at play.

Play — A Child's Work

Play:
It's the work of a child
Self-absorbed, content and mild.
Play:
It's the way children learn
About self and world,
Taking practice runs without concern.
Play:
It becomes an ignition key
For the motor that drives imagination,
Thought, reason, and creativity.
Play:
It will eventually evolve
Into games with goals to achieve,
Rules to follow, and problems to solve.
Play:
A child's work.

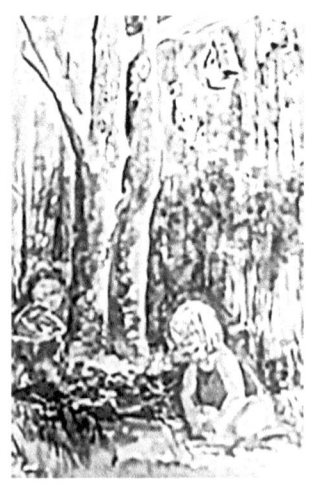

Flexibility

Creativity is essential for solving problems.
When an idea strikes, act on it.
Be confident — take risks.
Be playful — have fun.
Stay focused.
Get out from under the clouds.
Challenge biased thinking.
Harness your natural energy.
Connect the unconnected.
Shift points of view.
Try seeing with a global perspective:
Wonder why something is as it is.
Ask where in the world it is.
Locate it on the map, is the climate cold or hot.
Ask when that was, before and after what.
Think globally, act locally.
Try taking a different point of view.
Drink from someone else's cup.
Stand in someone else's shoes.
Try on someone else's hat.
Try on someone else's tee.
Flexibility in thinking leads to
Creativity in action

We All Wear Different Tees

Tee shirts
Almost everyone wears them
At one time or another
Sometimes they tell others who we are
Father, mother, sister, brother
Aunt, uncle, grandparent
Sometimes they identify the group we belong to
Sometimes they bear messages
About what we value
Our desires
Our beliefs
Our ideals
How we feel.
So, What's on
Your Tee?
Now try wearing
Someone else's tee.
How different might your actions have to be?

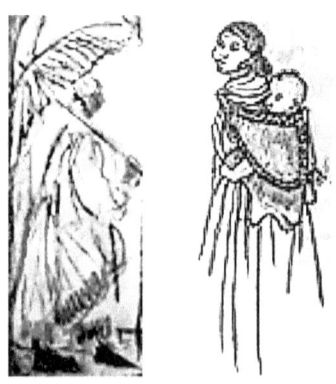

Walk in someone else's shoes

Art from Deep Down Inside

To live we must act.
To act we must make choices.
To make choices we must have a code of values.
To have a code of values
We must know who we are and where we are.
To know who we are does not mean what we look like.
Knowing who we are means understanding
Our inner nature, our inner world.
Likewise, knowing where we are in the world
Goes beyond describing the physical space we occupy
Or the groups to which we belong.
To validate and control our inner yearnings,
Fantasies, dreams, fears,
We need to understand the ways
Of the universe in which we act.
Art is something more than a representation of
An external physical world.
Art is rooted in the spirituality, beliefs, and values
Of our varied human experiences.
There may still be a few of us who believe that
Art does, indeed, come "from deep down inside."
Art can be an expression of our sense of life.
It is subject to an aura of mystery, faith, and awe.
It mirrors who we are and where we have been.

Searching for Common Ground

Why do people go to war?
Why do we focus on differences
When we have so much in common?
Why do we see things the way we do?
The answers can be found
On common ground
An amalgamated island of
Understanding and compromise
Within hand
But by choice and stand
Unreachable and untouchable
Isolated by
Intolerance, ignorance, indifference
Rigid, but not impenetrable,
Barriers to
Reason.

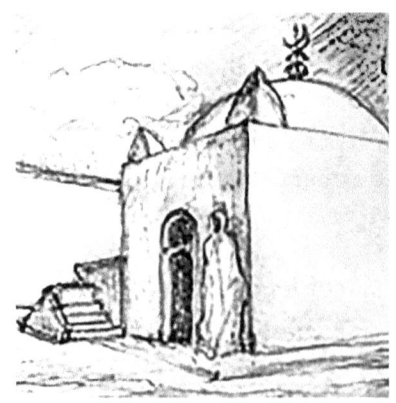

Mausoleum of Aw Hakim near Harar

The Ways We Were

Homo sapiens, we were, by ancestry,
Hunters and gatherers,
Seasonal wanderers out of Africa.
Homo sapiens, we were, by heredity,
Unsettled migrants,
Before we became, by necessity,
Productive farmers:
Shepherds of sheep, Winnowers of wheat,
Vintners of the vine,
Celebrating seasonal harvests.
Homo sapiens, we then became, by ingenuity,
Builders of permanent settlements,
Honoring family units, supporting community.
Homo sapiens, we have become, by destiny,
Designers of Hometown, a global village.

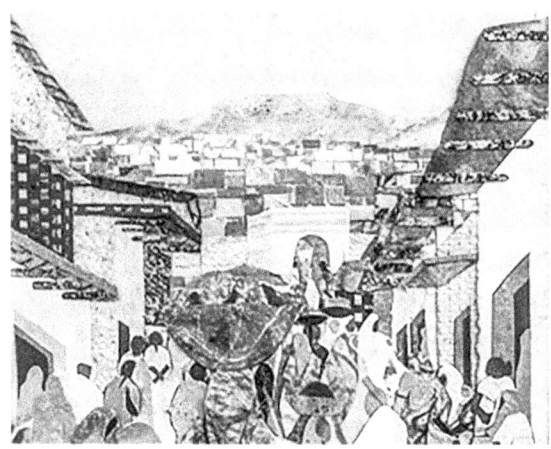

Hometown
Handmade paper

Hometown — A Global Village

We all live in Hometown
The whole wide world round
On mountain tops, in valleys, and shelters underground.

We all live in Hometown,
With someone just next door
In high-rise condos, low-rent flats, or cabins by the shore.

We all live in Hometown
Connected far and wide
Crowded close or spread apart
Yet dwelling side by side.

We all live in Hometown
Where the Internet's a fact,
Where people unseen
Unknowingly interact.

We all live in Hometown
Communicating with devices,
E-mails, E-vites, E-cards,
All — egads — tech vices.

We all live in Hometown
A Facebook mirage,
An imagined order
A faceless collage.

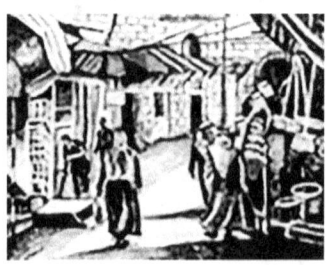

Amman, Jordan

We all live in Hometown
A tapestry of talents and creeds
With there and then dreams
With here and now needs.
We all live in Hometown
A safe haven of gentleness
Defined by kindness
Dignified with mindfulness.

We all live in Hometown
Where harmony is found
Where diversity is celebrated
The whole world 'round.

We all live in Hometown
With mosque, temple, church
Where heads bow in reverence
In one common search
To be the best we can be
To do the best we can do
For our actions matter most
Not for us, but for you.

We all live in Hometown
Where poetry and art
Draw us closer together
Setting differences apart.
We all live in Hometown — a global village.

Now — Worlds Apart

Tribal folk, we are
By nature
Wired
To be close to others
Connected
By a shared humanity
Social beings
Intended to help each other
To feed, to protect
To defend one another
To make sacrifices
For the sake of everyone's mother
Father, sister and brother
To trust and have faith
Yet
We live in a rapidly evolving society
Empowered by corporate greed
Far from egalitarian indeed
Cold, indifferent, alienating
Complex, technical, mystifying
A society at war with itself
A global village adrift
Now
Worlds apart
Yet
That's not who we are
By far

Complicated Lives

Oh, the anfractuous lives we lead
Complicated by the twisted words we heed
The tortuous rules we dare not break
And winding roads we are forced to take
Convoluted paths that too often turn
Into dead end runs with no return
Another day of endless toil
Another curve, another coil
Another loop, another bend
When will the flexuous downward spiral end?
You asked for an answer to this question, my friend
When will the flexuous downward spiral end?
The answer will twist and turn unbroken
Around what I have to say
The answer is found, not in work, not in play
But in the balance of life from day to day
So, I say in this most direct way
The end will be when we retire
To live the life, we were meant to live
Satisfied with the necessities
Not afraid of toil
Living life to its fullest
Breathing clean air
Nurturing healthy soil
Conserving fresh water
Living to give
Giving with love
Loving with care
Caring to learn
Learning anew

Retirement

In the years before retirement
We maneuver to make our mark
Driving in the fast lane, never shifting into park.
We slouch in convenience
Without concern for consequence
We marvel in the abundance of produce
Rarely considering how overproduction can reduce
Fertility of the land.
We surround ourselves with stuff
Without ever saying enough is enough.
We adorn ourselves with outfits for work and recreation
Without questioning if materialism is progress
Toward a greater destination.
We appreciate disposables and throw-aways
Ignoring the trash unchanged in landfills
And litter lingering along highways.
In the years after retirement:
We live the life we were meant to live
Living in balance, learning to give,
Satisfied with necessities, not afraid of toil
Loving clean air, clean water, and healthy soil.

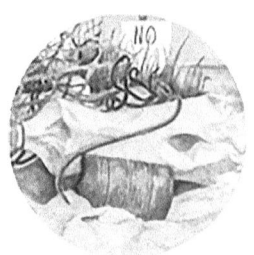

No Littering

A Poet's Metaphor

As life's journey begins its downward turn
We find ourselves with a patchwork of
Memories loosely stitched together
With short threads of imagination
Like scraps of fabric pieces
Randomly patterned and
Carefully sewn into
Colorful story
Quilts
That artfully
Reconstruct our
Bold footsteps taken
Strong desires forsaken
Sacrifices made for posterity
Hard choices made for prosperity
Beautifully crafted fabric creations
Hand-me-downs for future generations

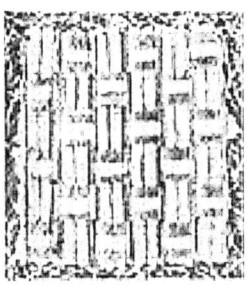

In Stitches
Handmade Paper

An Artist's Statement

For me, in the autumn of my life
Whether I am making, perceiving or reflecting
Art is an enjoyable exploration in crafting meaning
A personal journey to see, to find, to listen, to sense, to
feel
To bring forth the past, the forgotten, the overlooked
To give new meaning to the old, used and discarded
To watch the ordinary become so extraordinary.
When skill as dexterity becomes challenged
Words, images, and ideas can still be
Manipulated with energizing
Creativity and playfulness.
In the autumn of life
Craft matters still.
Skill matter too.
Tone matters
Most.

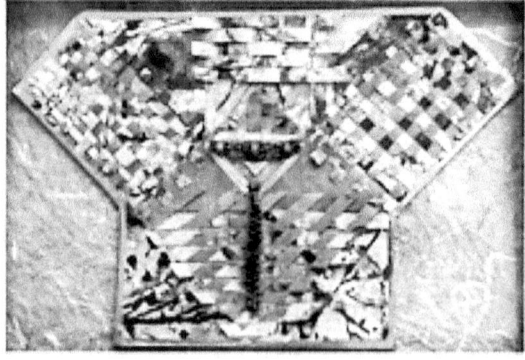

Clotho's Coat
Handmade Paper

First Person Singular

Singularly
I am confused.
The chairs are empty.
I am in a room by myself.
I know I entered for a purpose.
But now I have no memory of why.
Am I to be looking for something?
Is there a surprise party for me?
Me. Me. Me. It's all about me.
Am I the first person?
The first to arrive?
Am I special?
I forget.

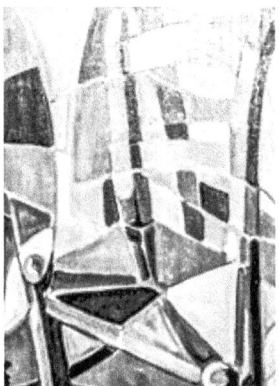

Empty Chair

I get confused.
Should I sit down or sit up?
Should I stand up or stand down?
Remembering comes in random spurts.
Details of facts memorized long ago are stark.
Trying to remember is like looking for my shadow in the
dark.

My memory condenses and combines.
My stories do not follow logical lines.
I often confuse times and places.
I can't recall names but see faces.
Truth spirals out of control.
Am I the first person
To see facts as fake this way?
On an okay day
If I think about my place in the world
I know I am part of a global village
Where I is we.
It's not me, it's us.
So why make a big fuss?
First person singular is overused.
Now we can all be confused.
So, get off your feet
Take a seat
Next to
Any of
Us.

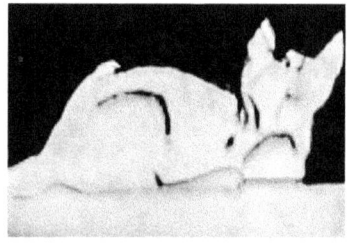

"Sorry, this seat is taken."

Third Person

Aged by years of hapless wandering
He sits in a garden he now calls home
She is by his side.
Weary from the heat and humidity
She remarks on the last day of summer
Her voice a mere sigh.
A gentle breeze through a jasmine archway
Sweeps the heady redolence
Of star shaped blossoms over them.

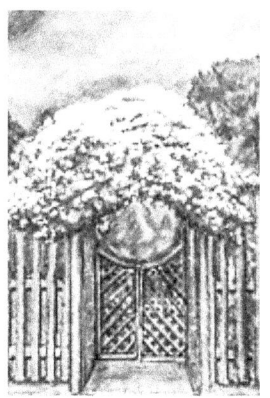

They watch the delicate petals dance
To the motion of harmless hovering bees
Collecting yellow pollen.
The lush white canopy comes alive
With the chirping of crickets hiding
In its tightly woven vines.
A small brown wren finds an opening
In the dense floral arch
And disappears.

Time passes . . .
He succumbs to the seductive jasmine perfume
Recalling a moonlit night along the Nile
More than a half century ago.
He strolls under the boughs of sweet jasmine
Alone in the shadow
Of a third person.
A shadow he will never see again
But will recall on the last day of summer
When jasmine is in full bloom.
Change goes unnoticed.
Fragments merge and meld
Into vague, flat shadowless shapes.
Fragrances blend, mix and evolve
Into mysterious infused scents.
The remains of the day
Pass in still quietness
One living form
Merging with
Another
Soon
To be
Unseen
In darkness.
Shadows fade.
The prophet prays.

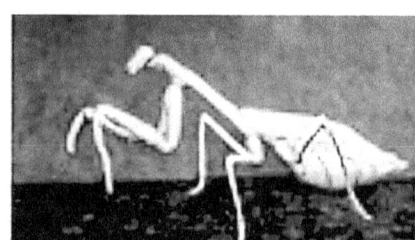

The Prophet

Contentment

If our intent is to be content
Three basic feelings become evident.
We must feel:
Competent at what we do,
Authentic thru 'n thru,
Connected with others
More than a familial few.
Contentment, we surmise
Comes not with money or status.
Contentment, we realize
Comes by having a community around us,
Solidarity grounded within us.
There can be no contempt
In contentment.

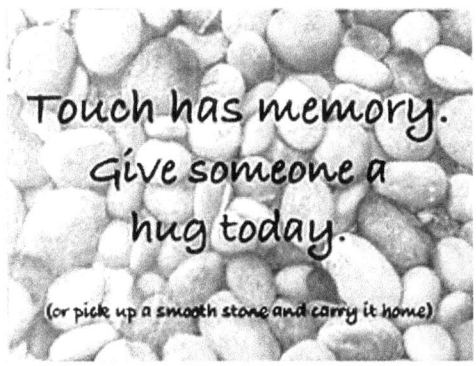

(or pick up a smooth stone and carry it home)

"One finger cannot lift a pebble."

MALI PROVERB

EPILOGUE

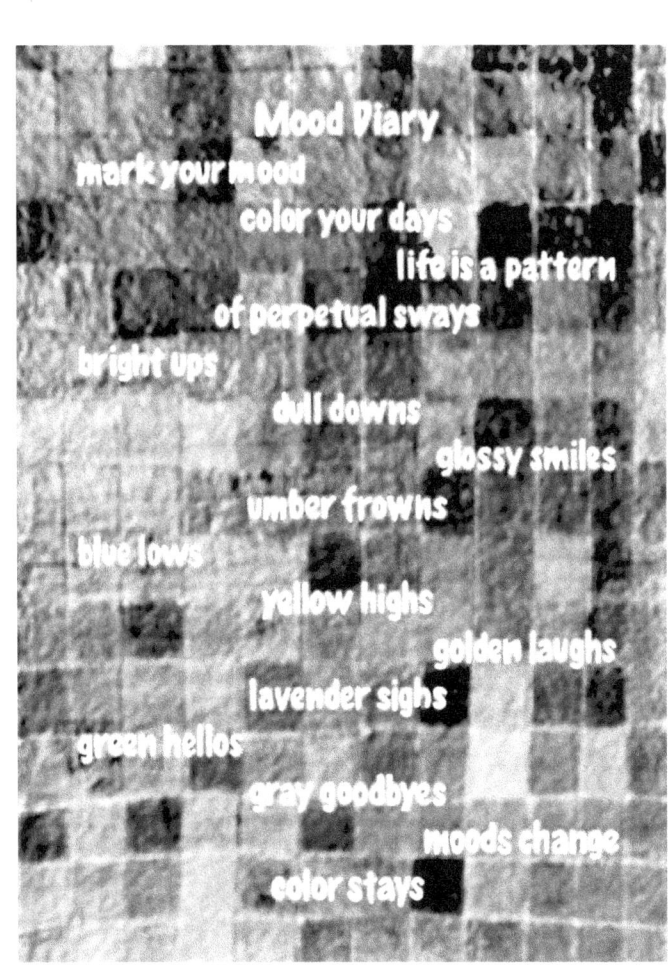

Mood Diary
mark your mood
color your days
life is a pattern
of perpetual sways
bright ups
dull downs
glossy smiles
umber frowns
blue lows
yellow highs
golden laughs
lavender sighs
green hellos
gray goodbyes
moods change
color stays

"Be not water, taking the tint of all colors."

MIDDLE EAST PROVERB

Final Reflection

We begin each new day
In the long shadow of our past.
We can move forward into the light
Or continue to look back to the vast
Accumulation of mistakes we've made
Opportunities seized; decisions delayed
Places we've been, people we've met
Projects we've not started yet.
Anticipating the future or
Dwelling upon the past
What will it be?

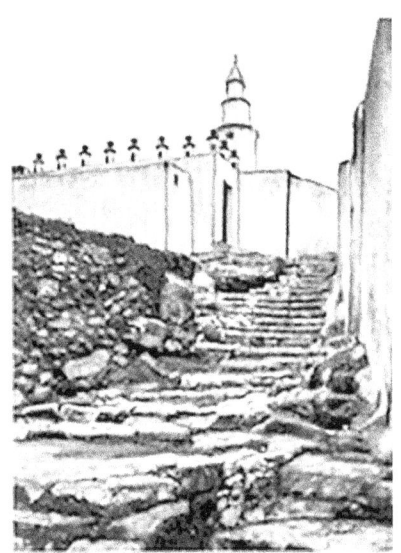

Back Street, Harar

We end each day
Reflecting
On hours
Passed
Wondering
If decisions made
Were really the best.
We put actions behind us
We will our body to rest and sleep.
If slumber escapes, we try counting sheep
Or we mentally walk the streets
Of the one place we loved
Remembering . . .

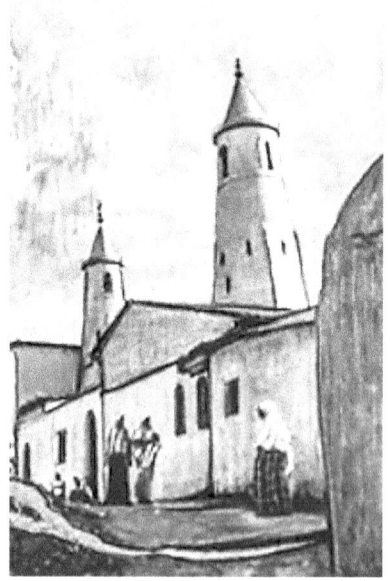

Side Street, Harar

We alone know the path our footsteps have taken.
But we may never know how, when or where
Our journey may have touched,
Or our actions awakened,
The lives of others
Unbidden.
Embraced by karma
We shape our destiny
Through small actions
Much like the flutter
Of butterfly wings.
Each negotiation,
Each reflection
Each nuance,
Each risk,
Moves us
Forth.
Day after day
Our actions initiate
Vibrations touching
Someone somewhere
Time and time again
As our journey comes full circle.

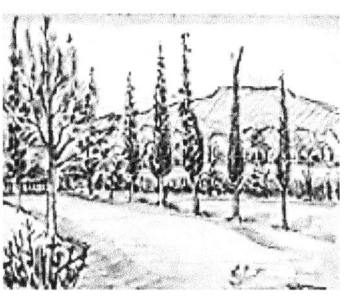

The road to our house in Harar.

Left only with poetry and sketches of memories
We become viewers of a graphite neighborhood
Hoping to glimpse traces of our footprints
That will take us back to see the good
Believing that time after time
Life touches life and
Above all else, our
Words matter
Especially
Tone
Far,
Far away
From home.

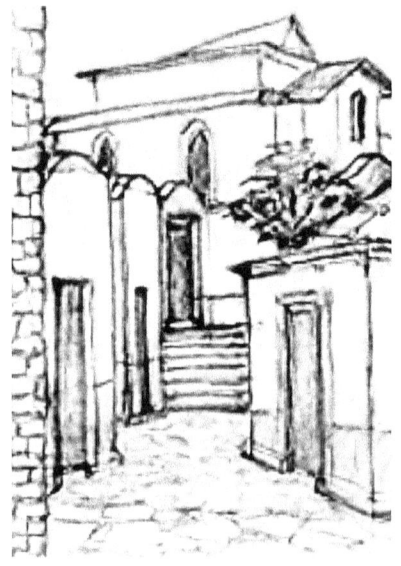

Cobblestone Passage, Harar

Far away from home,
Journeyers encounter
Sacred symbols of death
Reminders of their own mortality.

When difficulty confronts us
Spirituality comforts us
Humanity consoles us
Sanity compels us
To anticipate
What awaits.
Hopefully
Not quite
Yet.

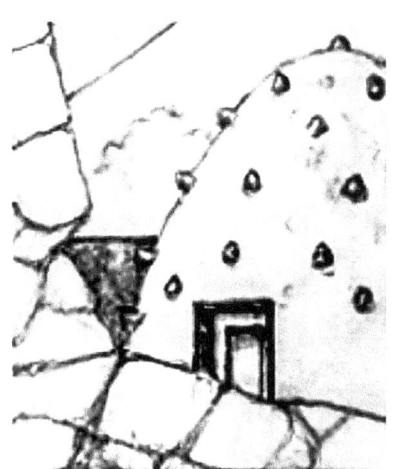

Tomb of Emir Nur, Harar

Unremembered moments
Of life harbor within
Voids that hold
The secrets
Of our
Faith
Or
Fate
As we
Struggle
For redemption
Unstuck in neither
Time, place or situation.
Secrets of indiscretions
Atoned for so very long ago
Remain hidden, safe and secure
Locked in the catacombs of repressed memory.

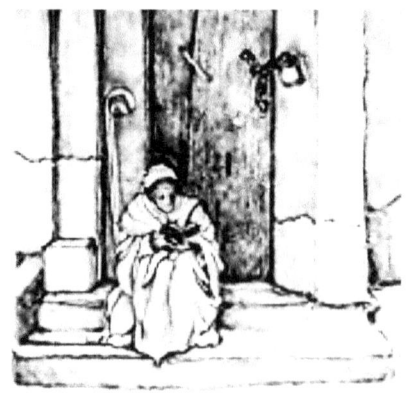

Locked Church. Lalibella

Now Worlds Apart

Tribal folk, we are
By nature
Wired
To be close to others
Connected
By a shared humanity
Social beings
Intended to help each other
To feed, to protect
To defend one another
To make sacrifices
For the sake of everyone's mother
Father, sister and brother
To trust and have faith
Yet
We live in a rapidly evolving society
Empowered by corporate greed
Far from egalitarian indeed
Cold, indifferent, alienating
Complex, technical, mystifying
A society at war with itself
A global village adrift
Now
Worlds apart
Yet
That's not who we are
By far

An Octogenarian's Claim

I'm well over eighty. I'm good.
Today's moments:
Sights, sounds, smells, emotions, touches
Sensory fragments to appreciate.
I'm good with that.
Creative thoughts:
A spark of an idea for this, a spark of an idea for that
Nothing whole or concrete, nothing orderly or complete
Just pieces to process and assimilate.
I'm good at that.
Daily reminders:
Don't be held hostage by the past.
Yesterday's solutions are neither today's nor tomorrow's.
Don't worry about tomorrow
Tomorrow will happen regardless.
Don't harbor regrets, forgive past hurts and sail on.
I'm good for that.
Morning mantras:
Flow with the current
Like water over river rocks
Breathe deeply, exhale slowly,
See beauty, feel love,
Make the most of what matters most:
Today's moments.

With dignity at eighty
I'm good enough.
I'm a Returned Peace Corps Volunteer.

ABOUT THE AUTHOR

Now and Then

Now

In the 21st Century, Eldon Katter identifies as an octogenarian, husband, father of three, grandfather of five, poet, papermaker and gardener. Notebook and a few paper-making supplies on hand.

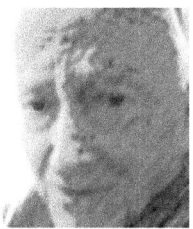

Selfie, 2017

Then

In the 20th Century, Eldon was Professor of art education at Kutztown University in Pennsylvania. He was also editor of *School Arts* magazine, and president of the National Art Education Association.

In the 1950s he taught art in Park Ridge, Illinois and later in Needham, Massachusetts.

As Peace Corps volunteers in the 1960s, Eldon and his wife, Adrienne, taught at a teacher training school in Harar, Ethiopia, and then worked for the Teacher Education in East Africa Project in Kampala, Uganda. Sketchbooks and journals in tow.

Self-portrait 1965

"Writing is the mother of eloquence
And the father of artists."

A SYRIAN PROVERB

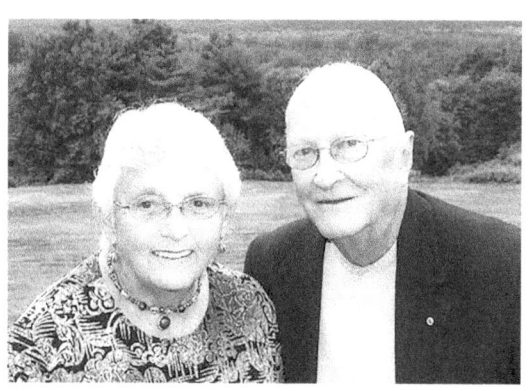

Eldon Katter and his wife Adrienne Damon
Katter were Peace Corps Volunteers in
Harar, Ethiopia from 1962 to 1964. Both
were training elementary school teachers.
They now live in Pennsylvania.